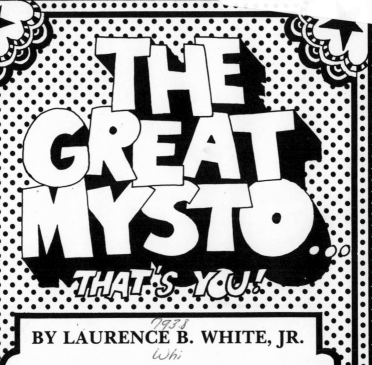

THE GREAT MYSTO...

THAT'S YOU!

793.8
BY LAURENCE B. WHITE, JR.
Whi

ILLUSTRATED BY WILL WINSLOW

▲

ADDISON-WESLEY

AN ADDISONIAN PRESS BOOK

Text Copyright © 1975 by Laurence B. White, Jr.
Illustrations © 1975 by Addison-Wesley Publishing Company, Inc.
All Rights Reserved
Addison-Wesley Publishing Company, Inc.
Reading, Massachusetts 01867
Printed in the United States of America
First Printing

HA/HA   9/75   08612

Library of Congress Cataloging in Publication Data

White, Laurence B
  The great mysto . . . that's you!

  "An Addisonian Press book."
  SUMMARY: Instructions for performing a variety of
magic tricks and presenting them to an audience.
  1. Conjuring—Juvenile literature. 2. Tricks—
Juvenile literature [1. Magic tricks] I. Winslow,
Will, illus. II. Title.
GV1548.W47   793.8   74-14743
ISBN 0-201-08612-3

CONTENTS

Contents

6/THE GREAT MYSTO ON STAGE   174

*A real stage show, a line of patter, to leave
the audience mystified and amazed.*

To Johnny Sisson . . .
Magician, Clown, Puppeteer, Comedian
. . . whose Pollylops, Stiplicks, and three-stair hops
have brought sheer delight
to thousands of children
like me.

CHAPTER ONE

BEFORE YOU BEGIN...

Have you the makings to be Mysto the Magician? Can you learn a trick, show it in an entertaining way, and keep the secret? Try this simple experiment: learn the two tricks that follow and try them on some friends. If you enjoy their reactions, and you have fun doing them, then you may indeed be The Great Mysto.

MAKING GEORGE FLIP HIS HEAD

You show a dollar bill lying on the table. Point out that the portrait of George Washington is right side up. As you talk, you begin folding the bill in half.

"George Washington was usually a real level headed guy, but there was one dance he really enjoyed."

You pick up the bill in the center of the folded side and begin to twist it end for end.

"Yes, sir, it seems ol' George really enjoyed doing the 'twist' and, most surprising of all," you say as you lay the folded bill back down on the table, "it seems that whenever he did the 'twist' he really flipped his head."

With that, you open the folded bill and the portrait of Washington is now upside down!

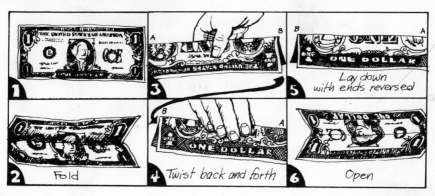

How?

Easy, but you must practice it a few times first. Follow the illustrations and it will seem to happen all by itself.

First fold the bill in half the long way. Be sure the portrait is right side up. Make your fold by bringing the top half down over the bottom half.

Now pick up the bill by grasping the middle of the folded edge. Be careful not to turn it around or people will think you are turning it upside down.

Lift the bill off the table and begin to twist it end for end as you tell your story. All you really do is flop the right end over to the left and then back again. Do this several times. (If you count the twists you make, you should always end up with an odd number of twists.)

When you put it down, and here is the whole secret, be sure you set it down twisted over. That is, the right end should be on the left.

The trick is done. You have actually turned the bill upside down right in front of your friends' eyes, but they did not see you do it because you did it in two steps instead of just one. Open the bill and see!

The story you told was a foolish one. Perhaps you can think up a better one. Just remember that a magician does more than just tricks. He must entertain his audience, too.

Some tricks require special equipment you will have to prepare yourself. You can make up the cards for this second trick as simple or as fancy as you like—they will still be very puzzling.

JUST THINK OF A NUMBER

You hand your friend five cards covered with numbers. You say, "On these cards you can find any number you like from 1 to 21. Sometimes you will see the number on more than one card. Would you look through the cards and think of any number you see."

Looking through the cards, your friend chooses one number.

You then say, "Please, just think of the number. Now would you look through the cards and give me all of them that show the number you are thinking of."

He hands you a few of his cards, and you glance at them very briefly.

You finish the trick by saying, "Would you please concentrate on the number. Ah, I see it now, you are thinking of _____ ." And, it really doesn't matter what it is because you will always name it properly—and you can do it over as many times as you like.

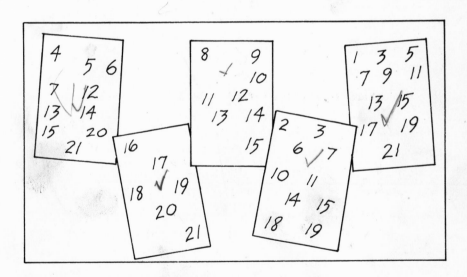

How?

This kind of trick is called a "self working" trick because everything is done for you automatically. In fact, all you have to do is be able to add in your head.

Would you like to see how the trick works right now? Think of any number between 1 and 21 and find all the cards in the illustration that show it. Now just ADD UP THE NUMBERS IN THE UPPER LEFT HAND CORNER OF EACH OF THE CARDS THAT SHOW THE CHOSEN NUMBER. The total will be the number!

You can make the cards big or small, plain or fancy; just be sure you put the same numbers on each card as shown in the illustration.

These are two quick tricks that practically do themselves. If you enjoy them and crave to learn more complicated things that will really bamboozle your friends, then you've been bitten by the magic bug and your only hope for a cure is to read on.

CHAPTER TWO

MYSTO AT MEALTIME

"So you're a magician? Okay, then show me a magic trick!"

There you are. You, The Great Mysto, without your rabbit, your expensive equipment, or your charming assistant. You probably don't have a piece of rope, red silk scarf, or the fancy new "Inside-out Square Egg Trick" you just got in the mail from the magic supply company.

So, can you meet the "show me a trick" challenge, or will you just stand there and watch your wand droop?

Impromptu magic is Mysto's greatest challenge. You certainly are not on the stage most of the time. But can't a magician do magic anytime? Magic certainly is not turned on and off like a water faucet. If you really are Mysto the Magician you must be "on" all the time, ready for anybody. What's more, you must do your impromptu magic with whatever is at hand—paper, scissors, handkerchiefs, salt, playing cards, and such.

Perhaps you will find this kind of magic the most fun of all. Many magicians specialize in "after dinner" or "close-up" magic done with their audience breathing down their necks. They love it because it seems impossible to fool people who are watching so very closely. Remember, closeup, a vanishing coin can amaze a person just as much as an elephant vanishing from a large stage.

Get ready to do closeup tricks. Every magician is asked to sometime. Get ready in the same way you get ready for a large stage show. Practice, practice, practice . . . then practice pretending that you are "taken by surprise" when someone asks!

Prepare a few tricks. Remember, the person who asks, "Show me a trick," is not asking for a half-hour show. Do just two or three and stop. Leave your audience wanting more. You have proved that you are indeed Mysto the Magician . . . and that is all you were really asked to prove.

This chapter is full of tricks you can choose from. Do not try to do them all, but choose a few that appeal to you and learn them well. They all use common items that are easily obtainable.

For an opening trick use a bit of comedy. This will get your small audience in the proper mood and wake them up for more amazing things. A bit of foolish mind reading works nicely.

TWO MINDS IN TUNE

Mysto jots a message on a piece of paper and lays it on the table with the written side down. He turns to a spectator and says, "Before I show you a magic trick, I would like to be sure our two minds are in tune. I would like you to study that piece of paper and tell everyone here exactly what is written on it."

The spectator thinks for a moment, looks puzzled, and says, "Gee, I don't know."

"Then you are absolutely correct," says Mysto as he flips the paper over to show I DON'T KNOW written across it in bold letters.

"Now that we have proven that great minds like ours do indeed think alike, we are ready to move on to some harder tricks," Mysto says as he ends his first trick.

How?

Naturally, there is no real trick here, just a quick joke on your audience. It will show everyone that you do not take yourself too seriously, and they shouldn't either.

If the person does not say, "I don't know," but tries to guess a word, just act very disappointed and keep saying, "You mean our minds are not yet in tune? Try again." He will eventually give up and say, "Then I don't know" . . . and the audience will laugh even louder when they catch on to what you have been trying to make him say!

If you, or your audience, are a bit disappointed that this is not a "real" mind reading trick, then you might follow it up with this next trick. This, your viewers will discover, is considerably harder to solve.

I'LL TOOTH-PICK YOUR MIND

Mysto tosses a handful of toothpicks on the table, turns his back, and says, "Please remove any number of toothpicks between one and ten and place them in your pocket so I cannot see how many you select."

This is done. Mysto still does not turn around.

"I'm having a bit of trouble picturing in my mind the number of toothpicks you have selected. Your mind seems cluttered with odd thoughts," Mysto says, "I see now, you're worried about your girl friend and you think she is going out with your best friend. Just so we can finish this mind reading trick, let me assure you that she is NOT going out with your best friend . . . as a matter of fact you don't even know the name of the boy!"

The audience laughs a bit.

"Perhaps I can help you concentrate more on tooth-picks and less on girl friends," Mysto continues. "Please count the toothpicks that are left on the table. I know there are ten or more. Now, take away enough toothpicks to represent the number. For example, if you have 11 left, take away one and one. If you have 14, take away one and four. If you have 18, take one and eight. Place the number of toothpicks you have taken away with the others in your pocket. Now, from the toothpicks that remain on the table, select any number you like and hold these closed in your hand. Put any toothpicks left on the table in the hand I have behind my back so I can use them to concentrate with. Now, please think about the number of toothpicks in your pocket and in your hand."

"Oh, I see you are thinking about girls again," Mysto says. "You sly old fox. I see you really have two girls, a blonde and a redhead, and you are trying to decide which one to invite out on a date. Well, I can tell you that the redhead will be the lucky one . . . because you're going to invite the blonde."

"Now that is cleared up, I can see a big number 11 in your mind," Mysto says going on with the trick. "Would 11 be the number of toothpicks in your pocket? And I see a four. Would four be the number you are holding in your hand?"

Mysto is right. His assistant is amazed!

How?

First, be very casual when you do this trick. Do not let on that numbers are at all important, even though they are, because this is a mathematical trick. You can use any *patter* you choose. A patter is a performer's chatter, conversation, or story. Some jokes, like Mysto's, are important to keep the audience's minds off the numbers.

You can use toothpicks, sugar cubes, paper clips, pennies, or any small objects. Just be sure you begin with exactly 20 of them. Again, don't let on that you are using any special number . . . be an actor . . . but start with exactly 20!

Follow Mysto's routine above. Turn your back and have any number of toothpicks between one and ten (this is important) placed in a pocket.

The spectator then counts the toothpicks remaining on the table and removes enough to represent that number (1 + 1 for 11, 1 + 2 for 12, 1 + 3 for 13 and so forth) and adds that number to those in his pocket.

This is followed by removing any number from those remaining on the table and holding these in his hand. The toothpicks left on the table are handed to you behind your back.

You can now, simply by counting those you are handed, tell exactly how many are in his pocket and in his hand!

How? Well, if you have done it correctly, he will always have 11 in his pocket! (So you can't repeat the trick too often.) And those in your hand and his hand added together will always make nine. Simply subtract your number from nine and you know how many he is holding.

Why? Actually it is simple subtraction. Get some objects and try it right now and you will quickly catch on. The "magic" is in removing enough "to represent the number." When this step is completed you will always have nine objects remaining on the table, and 11 in the pocket. Try it and see!

With closeup magic, "change of pace" is very important. Use different kinds of tricks, with different objects, to prove that you are indeed a real man of magic. It also makes it seem as though you can do magic with anything you touch.

ZIP CLIP

Mysto hands half a dozen paper clips to each of two spectators. He asks them to clip the paper clips together to make two chains.

"Watch and see how long it takes them," suggests Mysto.

The spectators finish and Mysto takes the chains from them.

"Boy, are you ever slow," he announces, shaking his head. "If I may use your two chains, let me show you how quickly a magician can link them."

He removes a dollar bill (or a strip of paper) from his pocket and folds it into a zigzag shape. He clips on the two paper clip chains, each on opposite ends.

"Would you each hold an end of the bill?" Mysto asks. "Now, with a touch of magic I will link the chains together faster than the eye can follow. On the count of three, pull the ends of the bill apart quickly and try to watch the chains melt together. One . . . two . . . three!"

The clips snap and the two chains are linked into a single one.

How?

You can practice this trick with just two clips. Later, when you try the trick described above, you will find it works the same way.

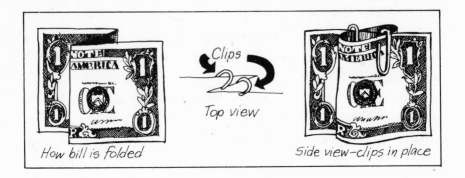

How bill is folded

Clips

Top view

Side view—clips in place

Study the illustration. Fold the bill back and forth in a zigzag in the middle. Be sure both ends stick out a bit.

The clips go on in a special way. One clips on the front with one end going inside. The other clips on the back with one end going inside. The illustration should be followed closely. If you have them on correctly the trick will work itself; if they are wrong it simply will not work at all.

Just pull the ends of the bill in opposite directions so it straightens out. The clips will slide together and link into a chain. It's easy and a real surprise.

By asking the spectators to make the first chains, the audience will later think that you did much more than simply link the two together. The longer chains help make a little trick look much bigger than it actually is!

Perhaps you might think of a way to "jazz" it up even more. You might use giant paper clips, a longer piece of paper, or a brightly colored ribbon. You can make the trick as showy and flashy as you like . . . or it can be a real after-dinner trick with a few borrowed paper clips and a borrowed dollar bill.

Closeup tricks should be short, with plenty of action, and should puzzle people as they go along. If people wonder what is going to happen they will be entertained. Naturally, the "end" should surprise them and please either their curiosity or their funny bone. The next two tricks will give you examples of each kind of ending. First a funny one . . .

CUT ACROSS

"I'm going to give you a quick little paper cutting lesson," says Mysto as he begins to fold a sheet of paper in various ways. "The trick will not sound very interesting. I call it my 'Cut Across' trick. I am simply going to teach you how to cut across this piece of paper."

Now he has finished with his folding. He picks up a pencil and draws a line across the folded sheet. The sheet, with a pair of scissors, is handed to a spectator.

"Here. Now let me see if you can cut across properly. Just cut along the line."

The helper snips the paper into two parts, each one still folded up. When opened up, one part falls into a number of small pieces.

"No, no," scolds Mysto jokingly, "You certainly didn't cut across that one, did you?"

Mysto begins to open the other folded slip. He stops, looks very pleased, and says . . .

"Ah, that's better. Remember when I began this lesson I said I would show you how to cut across with this paper? Did you think you already knew how to cut across? Well, without my help, did you know how to cut A CROSS like this one?"

He opens up the sheet completely to show that his helper really did cut "across," for the paper is in the shape of a church cross!

How?

It's not really a magic trick as you and your audience will soon decide, but it is an intriguing "quicky" that is cute and funny. Later, when someone tries to duplicate your folds, they may not find it very easy. Cutting a four-armed cross

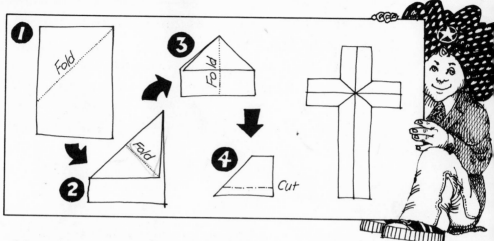

with a single scissor snip does require a tricky bit of paper folding.

It is easily learned in minutes from the illustrations. Just get some scrap paper, about 5½ by 8½ inches (exactly half a sheet of typing paper), and a pair of scissors, and do it over and over until you master it. Then you can do it every time . . . quickly, so nobody will remember how you folded it.

The next trick seems nothing like this one, but it has many of the same qualities. It is quick, keeps people interested, and has a fine ending. It, however, is not really an impromptu trick. You will have to get it ready beforehand.

COIN IN THE BAG IN THE BOX

"May I borrow a $100 bill please?" asks Mysto. "How about a $50 bill? . . . A $20? . . . well, how about a quarter, dime, or a penny?"

He is handed a coin. Mysto flips it high into the air and catches it with his hand.

"Ooops," he says, opening his hand and finding it completely empty. "I'm afraid that I have never been able to hold onto money very long."

The magician reaches into his pocket and removes a small cardboard box. He hands the box to the person who loaned the money and requests him to open it. The box is opened, which is difficult because there is sticky tape all over holding it closed. Inside is found a tiny cloth bag closed tightly with a rubber band. The rubber band is removed and the bag is opened. The missing coin is found inside! Mysto, who has been standing to one side while the spectator opened the box and bag, is delighted.

"I have never been able to hold onto money very long . . . because I am always in too much of a hurry to get it into the bank," explains Mysto as he turns the box upside down to show the word BANK written on the bottom.

How?

First, it IS the same coin. You can have your helper make a mark on it with a pencil, or simply remember the date if you wish.

The actual trick has two parts. Both will require practice on your part. The practice will be well worth it. When you do both parts together you have the makings of a miracle.

First, you must flip a coin and make it vanish. You *must* wear a jacket to do this . . . a sport coat, suit jacket, or fancy tuxedo. (Magicians are always well dressed!)

Flip the coin high into the air. Reach up as it falls back down. Hold your arm as shown in the illustration and close your hand around the coin as it touches it . . . but do not catch the coin. Simply let the coin slip through your hand and right down your sleeve onto your elbow.

It requires practice, but is surprisingly easy to learn.

Be sure to keep your hand closed as though it contains the coin. Turn toward your audience. Look at your hand. Convince everyone that it is in your closed hand. If you believe it, they will too.

Then . . . slowly . . . open your hand to show it is gone. Look puzzled. Be amazed with your audience. Turn your hand around slowly and study all sides. Finally, slowly, lower it to your sides as you shrug your shoulders.

As you lower your hand by your side, cup your fingers. The coin will fall right out of your sleeve and into your cupped hand.

Now that you have the coin back in your hand, what are you going to do with it? You must now get it into the sealed bag in the sealed box. This requires a bit of preparation. You must obtain several items.

First, a small cardboard box. A small matchbox is ideal. Or a small jewelry or "ring" box would be fine. Read how the rest of the trick works and you can then search for a box of the correct size. Once you find one it can be used over and over.

Next, a small cloth bag that holds a large quarter-sized coin easily. It is open at one end and is fairly deep. You can sew one up easily.

You will need a few rubber bands to go around the end of the bag. They should fit tightly, but not too tightly. You'll understand why as you read further.

Last, and most important, you will need a gimmick. A gimmick is that secret thing that the audience never sees or knows about. In this trick, the gimmick is a small flat plastic tube. You will have to make it.

Find a plastic vial about ¾ inch in diameter. Saw off the bottom to make a hollow tube. (Note: plastic vials are used to hold pills, are sold for coin collecting, hold bouillon cubes and toothbrushes.) Place the open-ended tube in boiling hot water for a few minutes until it becomes very soft. Remove it with a fork and lay it on a piece of wood. Press another piece of wood on top and squash the tube so that it is nearly flat. DO NOT squash it completely flat; you must leave it open enough for a quarter-sized coin to slide through easily.

Hold the wood on top of the plastic until it cools and hardens. You can pour cold water on it if you wish to speed up the cooling process. If you do not make it the right shape the first time, just place it back in the boiling water and soften it again. You can then open it with a table knife or squash it flatter until it's right.

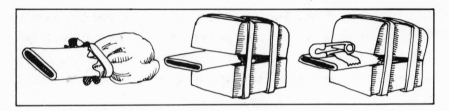

Now you're ready to prepare for the trick. Push one end of the flattened plastic tube in the bag and wrap a rubber band around it. Not too tightly!

Next, place the bag in the box with the tube sticking out. Wrap a few rubber bands around the box or stick on some sticky tape to keep it sealed closed. Do not stick any to the plastic tube. With sticky tape, fasten a safety pin to the top side of the plastic tube and pin this to the top of the inside of your coat pocket. With the tube-bag-box in your pocket, you are now ready for the second part of your trick.

Once the coin has fallen back into your hand, you immediately reach into your coat pocket, which contains the box. As your hand enters your pocket, simply drop the coin down the plastic tube. It goes directly into the bag inside the box.

Keep moving your hand down into the pocket. Pull the box downward and off the tube. The safety pin will hold the tube up while the box moves down. Once the box is free, remove it from your pocket, leave the gimmick behind and unknown, and hand the box to your helper. Step away and let him do all the opening. Your part in the trick is done and it's all over but the surprise.

If you wish, you can continue to coin-fuse your audience by borrowing the coin one more time for the "Finger Tip Gyp" or the "even if you feel it I can make it go" trick.

THE FINGER TIP GYP

Standing up, Mysto grasps a fold of cloth from his trousers and lays a coin on it. Quickly he folds the cloth up over the coin. He asks a spectator to touch the hidden coin with his forefinger.

"Can you feel the coin?" asks Mysto.

"Yes," answers the spectator.

"Would it be a miracle if I could make it vanish while your finger is on it?" asks Mysto.

"Yes."

"Then . . . Zingo . . . it is gone!" exclaims Mysto as he steps backwards, releases the cloth, and allows it to fall open showing that the coin has gone right under the spectator's fingertip.

How?

This trick is worth the practice it takes to master it. Once you can do the basic trick, as described above, you will discover its many other variations. You will also find it is a very handy way to make a coin vanish in other coin tricks. The illustrations will help you most of all. Look at them as you read the description that follows.

With your left hand, gather up a tuck of cloth on the upper part of your trouser leg. Keep your fingers toward your knee and your thumb toward your hip. Squeeze the fingers and thumb together with the cloth in between. Hold your thumb on top and the fingers under.

Hold the coin in your other (right) hand, between the thumb and first two fingers. Lay it flat on the fold. Hold it against the cloth with your right thumb and slide the fingers underneath the cloth and coin. Squeeze it in place and let go with your left hand. Show the coin under your right thumb.

Now, lift the fingers, while still squeezing the cloth and coin, and fold the cloth up over the coin. This hides the thumb and coin under the fold of cloth.

Your fingers are on top. At this point slide your thumb out from under the cloth and slip the coin right out along

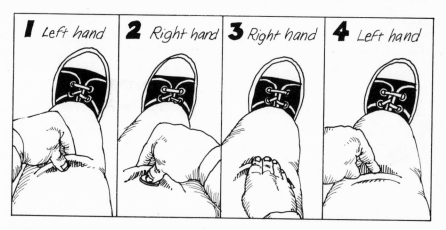

with it. Nobody will see the coin because your fingers, on top, hide it. Hold the coin against your right palm with your thumb.

Move your left forefinger down to the cloth and place it on top of where the coin should be. Pretend to hold it in place; actually all you are holding is the tuck of cloth.

Remove your right hand, holding the hidden coin. Keep looking at the cloth; if you don't pay attention to your right hand, nobody else will either.

While everybody is looking at the tuck of cloth, suddenly release your left finger and let it fall open. The coin is gone. At this same instant, without looking, casually drop the hidden coin into your pocket.

This is basically how the trick works. Practice the moves very carefully until you can do them very smoothly; then you are ready to do it the way Mysto did. If you have read the above very carefully you know that your finger did not feel the coin before it vanished. How did Mysto allow a spectator to touch it right up to the moment it vanished?

Mysto placed a quarter in his pants pocket. When he gathered up the tuck of cloth he did it on his leg right over the pocket. Then he stole the coin out exactly as described above but he asked the spectator to feel it. What the spectator felt was the coin in his pocket. When Mysto stepped backwards, the fold fell open and the coin appeared to have vanished right under the spectator's fingertip!

What else might you do with this same trick? Put a quarter and a dime in your pocket. When you are asked to show a trick, remove them together with the dime hidden under the quarter. The audience sees only a quarter.

Place the double coin on the tuck in your trousers. Fold the cloth over, just as before, and steal out the quarter. Leave the dime in the cloth fold. This sounds much more difficult than it actually is.

As soon as the quarter is gone, ask a spectator to place his fingertip on the "quarter." Guide his fingertip to it so he presses it in the middle and holds the cloth in place. Tell him to press the coin hard while you pull the cloth open from both sides. Imagine his surprise when the cloth falls open and his finger is still pressing hard against the quarter . . . except somehow it has changed into a dime while he was holding it!

Playing cards, like coins, seem to be "part" of magic. Magicians are expected to be able to do amazing things with them. Mysto would certainly be ready to do a card trick or two if he were asked.

Many people know a "pick-a-card and I'll find it" trick. Many rely on special arrangements or on remembering a card that goes on top of the chosen one. Since Mysto is a real magician, he allows the free choice of any card and the deck to be then thoroughly shuffled before he finds the card.

This special "pick-a-card" is the one you are about to learn. You will find that it fools all of your friends who know a card trick of their own. Keep it your own secret.

AN IMPOSSIBLE CARD TRICK

Mysto has been invited to do a card trick and has been handed a deck. He shuffles the cards a bit, fans them out, and invites someone to take any one he wishes. This is done. Mysto takes the card back, without looking at it, and returns it to the deck. He begins to shuffle.

"Some people may be thinking that I am able to keep your card in a special place in this deck so I can find it later, and that I'm not really shuffling the cards. This is not true," says Mysto.

He hands the deck to a spectator and asks him to shuffle the deck. While this is being done, Mysto turns his back so he cannot see the cards at all.

Finally the cards are returned to him. Mysto begins to thumb through the cards.

"Are you satisfied that your card is thoroughly lost in the deck, and I now have no way of knowing where it is?" he asks.

The spectator nods to agree.

As he flips through, he removes a single card and tosses it facedown on the table and says, "Strange . . . as I was looking through the deck I suddenly got a tiny electric shock as I touched this one card. We magicians are very sensitive to these things, you know. I think it is possible that I got a shock this time because I touched this same card a short time ago. I really don't know what card it is, and I don't know what card you selected, but I would be willing to bet that both cards are the same one. What card did you chose?"

"The three of hearts."

"Aha, I knew it," says Mysto, flipping over the single card.

Naturally, it is the three of hearts.

How?

This trick appears impossible for several reasons: a spectator loans the deck, selects the card, returns it anywhere, and shuffles the cards as much as he chooses. How is it possible? If you wonder now, imagine how it will make your friends wonder when you do it for them.

There is one "magic moment" in performing this trick. It is carefully written into the description, but it probably went unnoticed by you because it sounded very natural. You can be sure it will appear natural to your audience, too. The "magic moment" is when Mysto takes the card back, without looking at it, and returns it to the deck. It is in this moment that the trick is done, because although Mysto does not look at the card, he does touch it! A little pre-trick preparation is required. Actually you can carry it with you wherever you go.

Take a small piece of smooth white cardboard and a soft pencil. Holding the pencil point flat, rub it back and forth over one side of the cardboard. This will coat it with a layer of graphite "lead" which will rub off very easily. Place this cardboard in your pocket with the rubbed side out. This, naturally, is done well beforehand and your audience never sees this gimmick.

Have a card selected and, while it is being examined and remembered, reach into your pocket and slide the tip of your middle finger across the rubbed surface of the cardboard. A layer of "lead" will be deposited on the tip. You do not need much, once across lightly will do fine. Then remove your hand from your pocket. Hold the fingertip down so nobody notices that it is a bit "dirty."

Ask for the card and hold your hand out to receive it. As the spectator holds it out to you, reach for it and take it with your fingers underneath and your thumb on top. Touch the face of the card with your "dirty" fingertip, and the trick is all but done.

Quickly return the card to the deck. You might ask the spectator where you should put it. Let anyone shuffle it, as much as they like. No matter how much the cards are mixed you will always be able to relocate the chosen card by looking for the pencil lead smudge on its face.

As you remove the card to place it on the table, slip your thumb across the lead mark and rub it off. Don't worry if it doesn't all come off, it will just look as though the card had been handled by someone with dirty hands. (By the way, be sure the deck you use has not really been handled by someone with dirty hands before you!)

For your magical vocabulary: When used this way, the pencil lead is called *daub* by magicians. Daub allows you to make simple work of a card trick that would otherwise be absolutely impossible. Daub belongs to magicians only. Never use this word with anyone else . . . they might ask you what it means. Isn't it amazing that The Great Mysto has to keep some words secret, too!

If you would like to make your card trick a bit longer or if you have some small children in your audience, you might like to try a funnier way of locating the chosen card. Just try reaching into your pocket and pulling out an "Instant Rabbit."

INSTANT RABBIT

Mysto has had a card selected from a deck, remembered, returned, and shuffled. The cards are now spread out faceup on a table.

"Would you mind if I did not even try to find the card? Instead, I will call upon the assistance of a magical friend of mine," says Mysto.

He removes his handkerchief and with a few folds produces a rabbit puppet on his hand.

"This is Longfellow, the magic rabbit."

Longfellow twitches his nose and flops his ears.

"Longfellow, can you find the selected card?"

The rabbit nods yes.

"Okay, then you look through them carefully.

The puppet shuffles through the cards, pushing them around. Some fall to the floor.

"No, no, Longfellow, I said look through the cards, not push through them . . . and please do it carefully. Take your time."

Longfellow stops shuffling through the cards spread on the table. He turns very slowly and stares at Mysto, and then he slowly turns back to the cards. He begins to look through them again, but very, very slowly.

"Oh, come now, Longfellow, we're all waiting. Can't you go a little bit faster?" Mysto says.

Again Longfellow looks up at Mysto slowly . . . stares . . . then turns back slowly to the cards . . . then he very quickly starts to fumble through the cards again, throwing them every which way.

"Oh stop it! Don't be a show-off. Just look through them the way you did in rehearsal and find the selected card."

The rabbit stops looking. He comes up to Mysto's ear and whispers something into it.

"Longfellow wants to know if you chose a cherry-colored card?" Mysto asks.

"No," answers the spectator.

Longfellow sadly shakes his head "no;" then he returns to look through the cards once again. He stops and returns to whisper again in Mysto's ear.

"Longfellow wants to know if you've ever heard of black cherries?" Mysto asks.

The spectator laughs and agrees that his card was a black one. Longfellow shakes his head "yes" and flops his ears from side to side. He quickly looks through the cards again. Suddenly he jumps on top of one card and flips it over.

"Longfellow seems to have found your card," Mysto says.

But the rabbit is busy turning still another card over.

"What's this? Perhaps that is your card?" Mysto says.

Longfellow is still busy, paying no attention to Mysto or his audience. He turns another card upside down beside the other two.

"Come now, Longfellow, the man chose only one card. Make up your mind."

By now it appears that the puppet is confused. He has turned still another card upside down, which makes a total of four.

"Are you going to find this gentleman's card or shall I blow my nose on you?" Mysto asks.

Longfellow whispers in Mysto's ear.

"Oh, it appears that Longfellow does know exactly what your card was."

Longfellow whispers again, then flips over the first upside-down card.

"Longfellow says that your card is a black card, like this one, but not a club. (The turned over card is the ace of clubs.) Is he right?" Mysto asks.

The person answers, "Yes."

Another whisper and another card is flipped over.

"Longfellow says your card is a spade, like this one, but it is not the ace. (The second turned over card is the ace of spades.) Is he right?" Mysto asks.

"Yes," agrees the spectator.

The rabbit claps for himself and whispers in the magician's ear. Then he flips over the third card. (It is the five of spades.)

"Longfellow tells me he was sure you were going to pick the five of spades, but that you were not smart enough to do it. Is he right?"

The spectator agrees that his card was not the five of spades. Again the puppet whispers in Mysto's ear.

"Aha, then Longfellow tells me that if you were not smart enough to choose the five of spades then you must have picked the ten of spades," Mysto says.

Longfellow flips over the last card to show it is the ten of spades.

"Is he right? Was the ten of spades the card you selected?"

The spectator agrees that it was.

"Then I certainly think Longfellow deserves a round of applause for being such a smart rabbit." (Longfellow bows and claps.)

"Now, because you are such a fine magician and so very handy to have around, I will put you back in my pocket until I need you to help me again with my tricks . . . or to blow my nose!"

Mysto flips the handkerchief off his hand tosses it up in the air, catches it, and places it back in his pocket.

How?

Longfellow is a simple hand puppet you can make from any standard man-sized handkerchief. Be sure it is a clean and freshly pressed one. Save one handkerchief to make into Longfellow and do not use it for anything else (like nose-blowing).

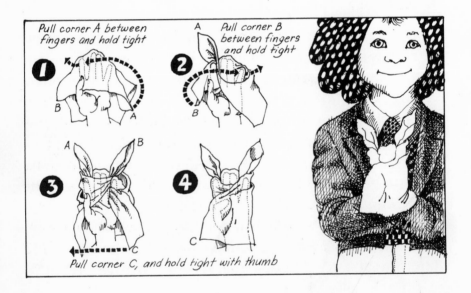

Use the illustrations to make Longfellow; then move your fingers inside to "bring him to life."

The routine suggested above is just a sample. The hand puppet can be used to help you with many tricks. Young audiences particularly enjoy him. Do not be afraid to make up a routine of your own for him. Be an actor, and make Longfellow an actor, too.

Here are some ideas that will get you started:

- He can "cry on your shoulder" if he makes a mistake.
- He can keep looking at a pretty girl, and you have to keep calling him back.
- He can "whisper in your ear" and then act embarassed because he is asking where the boy's room is.
- You can whisper in his ear to help him correct a mistake he's made.
- He can thumb through a magic book (How about this one?) to read how a trick should be done.
- You can make Longfellow on your hand by turning your back or holding your hands under the table. His sudden appearance is very appealing.

Naturally, it is always you, not Longfellow, who must do the trick. In the routine described above, you might use the daub method for locating the chosen card (see AN IM-

POSSIBLE CARD TRICK). It is then easy for you to spot the card when the deck is spread faceup across the tabletop. Once you know the selected card you can concentrate on acting. Remember that Longfellow's antics will be much more entertaining than simply finding a chosen card. Properly done, Longfellow will produce a few minutes of good fun and, later, leave your audience with the real mystery of how he really knew which card was picked. The real "magic" in this trick is your ability to bring Longfellow to "life." Practice that most of all.

Longfellow brings fun into a card trick, but perhaps you prefer a more serious mystery. If you want to convince your audience that you can do real magic, try this next card trick.

STRICTLY BY CHANCE

Mysto fans a dozen playing cards toward himself and studies them carefully.

"I am going to select six cards," he says, choosing them one at a time and laying them face down, scattered about the tabletop.

He hands the remaining six cards to a spectator, requesting that he not look at them.

"Would you place your cards one by one on top of the six cards I have laid down? You will make pairs strictly by chance because you don't know my cards or your cards."

The spectator pairs up the cards.

"Now, please point to any pair you choose," Mysto says.

This is done.

"Would you care to change your mind? Pick a different pair if you like. Remember, it makes no difference because this trick works strictly by chance."

The spectator makes his final selection of any pair of cards. Picking up the pair, Mysto flips them over to show their faces. He names them aloud.

"Strictly by chance these two cards came together to make this pair."

He replaces the pair facedown on the table, then gathers all the pairs up into a single stack. He hands the stack to the spectator.

"Now would you please deal them into two piles? Place a card first on one pile, then on the other."

This is done.

"Now," says Mysto, "let me show you how amazing 'chance' can be. What are the chances that you have separated the cards by their colors, and put all the red-colored cards in one pile and all the black-colored cards in the other? I would guess that the chances might be one million to one, wouldn't you?"

Mysto continues, "But, even more than that . . . remember the pile you selected. One card, the two of spades, was black and the other, the eight of hearts, was red. Remember those cards for a moment, because chance works in strange ways."

Pointing to the two piles, Mysto invites the spectator to turn them over and spread the cards out.

One pile contains all black cards . . . except for a single red one, the chosen eight of hearts! The other pile is all red cards, except for the black two of spades . . . the other selected card!

How?

Select any 12 cards from a deck for this trick, just be sure six are red and six are black. Fan the 12 cards toward you, pick out all six black cards, lay them facedown and scatter them about on the tabletop. Be sure nobody sees their faces and pick them out "carefully" and "deliberately" as if it were difficult for you to decide which cards to choose.

Hand the remaining six to the spectator, facedown in a pile. Tell him not to look at the faces because the trick must work "strictly by chance." Actually, you don't want him to see that all six are red cards!

Ask him to put one of his cards on top of each one of yours. This is really by chance, but he will pair a red card up with a black one every time.

Now he selects, by pointing, any pair. He may change his mind as often as he likes. When his final choice is made, pick the cards up, turn them over, show them, and name them. Ask that they be remembered. Now, when you turn them over the red card will be under the black one. As you show them, one in each hand, and put them back together, switch their order. In other words, put them back with the red one on top of the black one. This switch is what makes the cards "find" themselves later on, so it is a very important move.

Set this selected and reversed pair back on the table facedown, and remind people again to remember the cards.

Quickly now, pick up the pairs one at a time and stack them in your palm in a single pile. Be sure to pick up both cards in a pair and drop them on the stack together. Also, pick up the reversed pair about halfway through, and add that to the stack in your hand.

Finally, hand the single stack to the spectator, facedown.

Ask him to deal the cards, one by one, into two piles. Be sure he puts first one card in one pile, then the next card in the other pile.

Without knowing it, he is really placing all the red cards in one pile and all the black cards in the other . . . except for a single pair . . . the two cards you reversed. The two reversed cards will show up as the only wrong-colored cards in both piles.

If you do not completely understand how stacking, and not chance, makes this trick work, get some cards and try it yourself right now. After you see it work one time, you will understand it easily. Then try it on a friend. You will be amazed to see how such a simple trick can fool someone so completely . . . but it always does!

Some people get bored with card tricks, particularly if you do several in a row. Don't be afraid to toss in a funny bit of business to change the pace. The following, for example, will take you only 30 seconds.

THE FASTEST CARD TRICK IN THE WORLD

"Would you like to see the fastest card trick in the world?" asks Mysto the Magnificent while holding a deck of cards.

"Yes," his audience answers eagerly.

"Okay," says Mysto, without moving a muscle. "Now . . . would you like to see it again?"

This might be a good time, before someone throws something at you, to do something a bit more magical. A bit of humor, and a change from playing cards, might be in order.

THE SWIMMERS AND THE SOAP

Mysto begins to introduce his trick while he is filling a drinking glass with water.

"I would like to tell you something about water, children, and soap," he explains. "Please imagine this glass is a swimming pool filled with water."

He picks up a pepper shaker and sprinkles a light layer of pepper grains on top of the water.

"Next, please imagine that these little grains of pepper are tiny girls and boys swimming in the pool. You know that some mothers have an awful time when they try to give their children a bath. They often decide that their children just don't like the water. This is not true. Children love the water. Just look at how much our swimmers are enjoying it. What mothers don't understand is this: Children love the water; what they hate is the SOAP. I would like to prove this."

Mysto picks up a bar of soap.

"You can see all of our swimmers having loads of fun in the water, but watch what happens when someone tosses a bar of soap into the pool."

Mysto touches a corner of the soap bar to the water surface in the center of the pepper grains. Suddenly, mysteriously, all of the pepper grain "swimmers" rush away from the soap and gather along the very edge of the glass!

The audience laughs. You will, too, when you do it for the first time.

How?

There is no magic here. Just a funny idea, and a simple scientific experiment.

Water is covered by an invisible elastic "skin" called its surface tension. The pepper is sprinkled on top of this skin.

When soap touches the middle of the water surface, it breaks the surface tension. Like a hole in a sheet of tightly stretched rubber, the surface tension draws away from the center. The pepper grains on top are carried away with it.

You cannot see the surface tension, but you can see the pepper grains. It will appear that they did not like the soap and "swam" away from it. This, naturally, is what makes your story so funny.

All water has surface tension, except for soapy water. Be sure to use a very clean glass and fresh water for this trick. If the glass of water is at all soapy, the trick will not work.

Try it. Right now. Because it works all by itself, it will look like real magic even to you.

CHAPTER THREE

MYSTO GOES TO A PARTY

"Please come to my party, Mysto" is an invitation Mysto will hear many, many times. Parties are supposed to be fun and everyone knows that a magician can bring along a very special kind of fun.

Parties are fun for the people there, but they are not always fun for Mysto . . . unless he is ready with just the right kinds of tricks and he knows what to expect.

Our Mysto, though, has performed at many parties and he has learned many of the problems:

- The audience will be made up of people of many different ages, mostly small children, but parents will also be there.
- There is no stage so the audience will sit very close to you and all around you.
- There probably won't be anyplace to set up your equipment or anyplace to put it afterwards when all the kids are trying to paw through it.
- There will be a lot of noise. The audience may yell and shout at you. This is a party and parties are noisy!

How does Mysto solve these problems? How would you? By thinking about them ahead of time and preparing for them.

Select a great variety of tricks so everyone, young and old, will find something to interest them. Have mostly tricks that are short and a lot that are funny. Have some tricks that include helpers and some in which the entire audience can participate. Don't use anything dangerous, like knives, or anything young children do not understand, like playing cards. Select your tricks carefully for a young, excited audience.

Try to have your audience seated in front of you. One way to do this is to set up a table in one corner of the room and stand with your back to the corner. This way, nobody can get too far around you or behind you. If, however, your audience is all around you, try to choose tricks that have nothing secret that will show from the back.

Have a small suitcase in which to carry your tricks. Have them all arranged in order inside the case. When you get to the party, simply open the case on your table, do your show, and close the case when you're done. You can even print MYSTO THE GREAT on the cover and open that toward your audience. This keeps them from peeking inside, and tells your audience who you are.

Try to keep your audience as quiet as you can. Don't be afraid to ask an adult to help you quiet the audience down.

Everyone will have a better time if they can see and hear what is going on. Promise them if they are quiet you will let them help you with a trick. Later, they can help by shouting a magic word at the right time. Give them a time to be noisy, and a time to be quiet. Remember, though, parties are very noisy and you may just have to learn to do your wondrous magic in spite of it.

This chapter takes you to one of Mysto's party shows. It shows you the kind of tricks he does. If you wish to do the same show, use only a few of Mysto's tricks . . . the ones you like best. Fifteen minutes would be the best length for a party show. Do not try to do too many tricks or carry the show on too long. The thing that makes a party fun is doing lots of different things. Remember that you are just one of the fun things going on.

Now the party is on. Mysto is set up and has just been announced. His show begins . . .

MYSTO THE MAGICIAN HERE NOW

"Let me tell you a funny story," Mysto begins as he opens out a long strip of paper. "When I was first starting in this magic business I was afraid that nobody would know me, so I had this sign made up."

He opens the strip all the way. It reads:

MYSTO THE MAGICIAN HERE NOW

"One day I looked at the sign and decided it was foolish. Nobody should have to read all those words. Take the last word **NOW**. We don't really need that, do we? After all, if I am showing the sign, I must be here now. Let's get rid of it."

He tears off the word **NOW**.

"But, look at the sign now: **MYSTO THE MAGICIAN HERE.** Naturally I am here. You can see me holding up the sign so I must be here. What a waste of time **HERE** is. Let's get rid of it!"

He tears off the word **HERE**.

"Ah, that's better. **MYSTO THE MAGICIAN**. But wait a minute. Everyone knows that I am a magician. They invited me here to do magic so I don't really need that on my sign, do I?"

Mysto tears off the word **MAGICIAN**.

"Now will you look at this sign: **MYSTO THE**. Mysto the what? . . . Mysto the Midget? . . . Mysto the Rosebud?

. . . Mysto the Flat Tire? It really doesn't tell you, does it? Here, let me fix it."

He tears off the word **THE**.

"Now," he exclaims, "we can all understand the sign: **MYSTO**. That's me! So now our sign is doing just what it's supposed to do: telling you the name of the world's most famous magician."

Mysto stops, thinks for a moment.

"But wait, maybe I'm getting carried away. Not everyone knows that my name is Mysto and I am the world's most famous magician. Some people don't even know that I'm a magician . . . or that I'm really here . . . or really here right now. Ah, well. . . ."

He places all the pieces of the sign he has ripped apart into a bundle and squeezes them hard. Then he slowly opens them out.

". . . perhaps I was much better off with the sign the way it was in the beginning."

The sign is now whole again and reads:

MYSTO THE MAGICIAN HERE NOW

"At least this way you all know that my name is **MYSTO**, and that I am **THE MAGICIAN**, and that I am **HERE**, and that right **NOW** I would like to do some more magic for you!"

How?

This type of trick is called a *restoration*. You must restore, or return to normal, a piece of paper that was torn into pieces. It appeals to audiences because they know it is impossible, yet you appear to do it without even realizing what you are doing.

Cut two strips of paper 22 inches long and 4¼ inches wide. These are easily prepared by snipping two sheets of typing paper in half lengthwise and then taping two of the halves end to end with sticky tape on one side. On both strips, with a heavy black pen, print:

MYSTO THE MAGICIAN HERE NOW

Make the letters bold, easily readable, and exactly the same on both strips. (Naturally, you can use your own name if it's not MYSTO.) To get them identical, lay a blank strip on top of a lettered one and trace the letters.

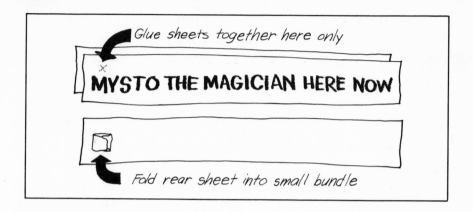

Put a little glue in back of the word MYSTO on one sheet and lay the back of the other sheet on top. Both sides show the printing out and are glued together only in the center toward the end with the word MYSTO.

When the glue hardens, fold one strip up into a small bundle behind the word MYSTO on the other sheet. When you hold up the sign with the words toward the audience keep the bundle on the back and nobody will be aware of it.

To perform, show the sign and tear off the words just the way Mysto did. Be sure to keep talking to keep your audience's attention.

Finally, gather up all the pieces you have torn off and lay them over the final word, MYSTO (which still has the hidden sign behind). Fold in the edges of the MYSTO square to form a bundle around the torn pieces. Squeeze the bundle tight so pieces will not fall out.

As you squeeze, simply turn the bundle over to bring the bundle made by the full strip to the front.

Continue with your story and slowly open out the "restored" sheet. When it is fully opened, the bundle of torn pieces will be hidden behind just like the full sheet was at the beginning.

Hold up the restored sheet in a matter-of-fact way. Do not act surprised or impressed that a trick has happened. Appear not to notice, but pretend this is "expected" and "happens all the time" . . . after all, you are Mysto, the world's most famous magician, aren't you?

If, after this opening, your young audience is still a bit unsettled and not paying strict attention, you might move on to a trick that calls on their ability to concentrate. Challenge them!

WATCH VERY CLOSELY

"A magician's job is to try to fool you. I am going to do just that," says Mysto. "Your job, of course, is to try not to be fooled. Let's see who is better at his job."

Mysto picks up a small cardboard box without a bottom and a paper cup containing a small rubber ball, and says, "Let me warn you. If you do not pay attention, even for a single second, you will be fooled. Let me try."

He shows the box completely empty, then sets it down on the table. He next drops in the ball, then puts in the cup.

"Now, if you have been watching carefully," he explains, "you will know that when I lift the box the ball must be beside the cup. This is so because I put the ball into the box before I put in the cup, right?"

Mysto lifts the bottomless box to uncover the ball and cup side-by-side as he said. He replaces the box and removes the ball and the cup.

"Now that you understand why you must watch carefully, let me do it again. But this time I will try even harder to fool you."

Mysto drops the ball into the box, then quickly drops in the cup.

"Is the ball inside the cup or beside it?" he asks.

"Beside it," answers the audience.

"Ah," responds Mysto, lifting the box to show only a cup sitting underneath, "then I guess you were not watching closely enough that time."

He tips the cup over to spill the ball out from inside.

"Perhaps you would like another chance?"

The audience eagerly agrees.

"First we drop the ball into the box. Then the cup. Now the ball could not possibly be in the cup could it?"

Mysto has repeated the same moves as before, with the spectators watching more closely this time. Still, when he lifts the box, the ball is found inside the cup!

"One more time?" suggests Mysto. "This time we will watch in slow motion."

Moving very, very slowly he drops the ball into the box. Then, very quickly he drops in the cup.

"I drop the cup quickly," he explains, "so you won't think I have time to sneak the ball into it."

Again, in slow motion, Mysto lifts the box to find just the cup showing. He lifts the cup, and slowly dumps the ball out of it.

"Now let me tell you the amazing secret of this trick," explains Mysto as he once again repeats dropping the ball, then the cup, into the box. "This trick works only when people are fooled by it. When the ball knows it is fooling you it will jump by itself into the cup."

Mysto peers down into the box and says, "Oh, oh, this is terrible. Now that I have told you how the ball works, it refuses to jump again. Now I just cannot do the trick any more."

The magician lifts the box and, sure enough, the ball is sitting on the table beside the cup. Mysto shows the ball, the cup, and the box and sets them aside.

How?

Most magic tricks should be shown one time and never repeated. This trick is an exception to the rule. To be effective it has to be done several times. Each time the audience looks a bit more carefully, so a "repeater" trick must be easy to do and very simple.

When doing a trick like this it is always tempting to repeat it many, many times because it is so easy to fool people with it. This is a mistake because you will only bore your audience. Never do it more than three or four times. Entertain your audience, intrigue them, arouse their curiosity, puzzle them . . . but never, never bore them.

You will require four things: a small brightly colored rubber ball (or an egg, handkerchief, pencil, magic wand, or any small object), a small cardboard box open top and bottom (decorate it any way you like), and two matching paper cups. The cardboard box should be taller than one of the cups and big enough so two cups and a ball can easily fit inside when placed side-by-side.

Begin with the two cups stacked together to look like one. Always call this "the cup." You must always let the audience believe that there is but a single cup used. This is the trick's secret.

Follow the above description of the trick to understand the moves you must make with the box, cup(s), and ball.

First set the box on the table and drop in the ball. Then drop the cup(s) in beside it. Lift the box and show the ball beside the cup(s). Pick up the ball and drop the box back over the cup(s). Immediately reach in the top of the box and lift out the cup. Really, remove one cup and leave the other inside. You now hold a cup and a ball. Drop the ball into the box (and right into the cup hidden inside).

Next drop in the cup you are holding. Just drop it. Do not put your hand into the box or people will suspect you moved the ball. Drop the cup beside the one already in the box.

Now you must lift the box, but you must lift the empty cup along with it. Just grasp the side of the box with your fingers and thumb and squeeze the cup, with your fingers, against the side.

Do this easily. The audience sees the cup sitting on the table and that attracts their attention. Set the box down on the table to one side. Lift the cup and show the ball inside.

You are then ready to repeat the trick immediately. An empty cup is already in the box. Drop the ball into the box (and into the cup); then drop the visible cup into the box after it. Lift the box, again lifting the empty cup away with it, and "discover" the ball that has somehow jumped back into the cup. Set the box, with the empty cup inside, down and you are immediately ready to repeat the trick again.

This is what makes this trick such a good "repeater." Each time you do the trick you also set it up so it can be immediately done again.

When you are finally ready to close out the trick simply drop the ball into the box beside the hidden cup. Then drop the visible cup into the box so it falls inside the hidden one. When you lift the box this time the ball will be beside the cup(s) and you are back where you began. Casually show the ball, the cup, and particularly the decorated box (because the audience usually suspects the trick is in the box) and set them all aside.

Usually a party is in somebody's honor. You, like Mysto, will be invited to many birthday parties. It is nice to acknowledge the person early in the show and even use him to aid you in a trick or two. Mysto's next trick does this and gives the birthday person a special treat, too.

CUPCAKE IN A HAT

Mysto invites the birthday person up to help him. He hands the boy or girl an old hat to hold and examine.

"When you're sure there is nothing inside the hat, will you give it back to me please?" Mysto says.

He then places the hat down on the table so it is bottom up.

"Did you get a magic cake for your birthday? No! You mean you just got a regular plain old cake? Well, we certainly have to fix that," Mysto says as he picks up a big paper cup full of confetti and holds it out toward the helper.

"A magic cake contains only three ingredients. First, just a little colored confetti. Would you take some from this cup please and drop it into the hat?"

The helper does this.

"Perhaps just a bit more," explains Mysto as he removes more confetti from the cup and drops it into the hat.

"Next, we need a little mixing," orders Mysto as he picks the hat off the table and holds it over the assistant's head.

"Would you hold the hat over your head and shake it back and forth."

The helper begins to do this.

"Our last ingredient for a magic cake is a little help from all the party goers. Will you all help us bake a magic cake by reciting out loud the most magical words we can say today . . . . Happy Birthday."

Together the audience shouts, "HAPPY BIRTHDAY!"

"Let's see how we all did. Would you lower the hat and take a look inside to see if our magical recipe has done anything?"

The birthday person lowers the hat he has been holding, looks inside, and removes a beautifully baked cupcake.

How?

This is a classic magic trick. Magicians have been baking cakes in people's hats for many centuries. It is an old, but always surprising trick. It seems as impossible today as it did when it was first performed.

Of course, like all good magic tricks, this one is really impossible. So it is up to you to sneak a pre-baked cupcake into the empty hat right under the audience's noses. This takes a little practice and nerve, but is really very easily accomplished.

The secret is in the paper cup full of confetti. It must be a large one, much larger than the cupcake. The cupcake, by the way, can be quite small . . . the surprise of finding it is the important thing.

Remove the bottom of the cup. Also cut a hole in the back of the cup near the bottom. See the illustration to see exactly where.

Next cut a circle of cardboard to fit about 3/4 the way up from the bottom inside the cup. Tape it in place.

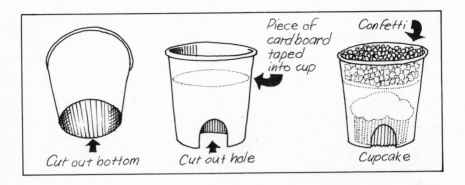

Cut out bottom   Cut out hole   Piece of cardboard taped into cup   Confetti   Cupcake

Fill the upper part of the cup with confetti. (You could also use sugar if you wished to bake a "sweet" cake.) Place the cupcake on the table and drop the cup of confetti over it. Keep the hole in the back of the cup facing the rear so it won't be seen. You are now ready to perform the trick. But practice, please, before trying it on an audience.

Use an old felt hat, or any old hat you can find. Hand it to a helper for examination and have it returned. Place it brim up on the table.

Lift the cupful of confetti off the table. When you do this, stick a finger in the hole in back and hold the cupcake in so it is lifted along with the paper cup.

Ask your helper to pick out a bit of confetti and drop it into the empty hat. As soon as he has done this, pick up the hat in your free hand. Say "I think we need a bit more," and start to sprinkle confetti right out of the cup into the hat. As you finish allow the bottom of the paper cup to lower into the hat. At this moment, release your finger-hold on the cupcake and let it fall right into the hat. Lift the bottom of the paper cup out immediately. Holding it high above the hat allow just a bit more confetti to be sprinkled into the hat. Then remove the cup and set it aside.

Hold the hat high so nobody can look inside. Hold it over your helper's head and ask him to hold it and shake it gently.

The trick is done. The shaking and magic words are just "frosting on the cake" to make the trick more entertaining.

If you buy a tube of cake decorating frosting you can write the name of your birthday person on the cupcake. This personal touch may make your 10¢ cupcake the most cherished birthday present he or she receives.

While you have the birthday person up with you it would be nice to allow him to help you with another trick. Mysto likes the following trick because it uses a helper and it is a sure laugh-getter.

I'LL MAKE YOU AN INSTANT MAGICIAN

While removing a length of rope from his suitcase, Mysto invites someone from the audience forward to assist him with a trick.

"Usually it takes years to become a magician. However, I have discovered a simple way to turn anybody into a magician instantly. We will use you . . . and this piece of rope."

Mysto holds the rope by one end, allowing the other end to hang down.

"By simply snapping this rope you will be able to magically tie a knot in the end. If you will allow me to make you a magician you will be able to perform this amazing trick right now. Are you willing?"

The volunteer nods his agreement.

"Then," exclaims Mysto, "Instant Magician!"

He steps behind the helper and thrusts his arms out under the volunteer's armpits. From the audience's view it appears that his arms belong to the helper. Naturally this is not meant to trick them, but they do laugh when they realize that Mysto's "Instant Magician" is simply his arms on the helper's body.

He waves the rope and his arms about while people are still realizing the joke; then he continues with the trick.

"Now that you are a magician, let's see you snap a magic knot in the end of the rope."

Mysto gathers the rope up in a loop and snaps it out. Nothing happens. Again he tries. Still nothing.

"Ah," he says to the helper, "you need more than magic hands to be a magician. You need a magic word. One of my favorites is 'Auntie ice cream.' Let me hear you say it."

The helper starts to say the magic word, but Mysto interrupts him.

"Not yet . . . wait until I, er, I mean you, snap the rope out. Do it when I say NOW, okay?"

Mysto coils the rope.

"NOW," says Mysto.

"Auntie ice cream," says the helper.

Snap goes the rope. And there, right on the end, is a very fine knot!

As he thanks his assistant, Mysto hands him the rope with the knot still on the end.

"Now that I have made you an instant magician, you might like to take this rope along so you can show all your friends the wonderful trick you did for us today."

How?

You can do this simple trick without using a helper, but you will find it is much better received if you try this comedy presentation. The basic trick of snapping a knot in one end of a length of rope is easy enough to do either way.

Here is how the trick is done. Tie a knot in one end of a four-foot length of clothesline rope, about three inches in from the end. This rope would be in your suitcase or somewhere out of sight.

In presenting the trick, pick up the rope, holding the knot hidden inside your hand with the other end hanging down. The audience should not see the knot, or know that it is there.

To snap the rope, simply pick up the end that is hanging down and place it in the other hand right over the knot. The rope now hangs in a loop . . . both ends being held in one hand.

Quickly snap the rope, like a whip, and as you do, release one end. If you release the end without the knot it will appear perfectly natural, and nothing will have happened. If, however, you release the end with the knot (you switch ends), it appears that a knot has suddenly appeared in the rope.

That is all there is to the trick, but practice it before trying it with your arms around an assistant. You cannot see what is happening while standing behind him so you will have to learn to do everything by the sense of touch. Naturally, because the audience finally sees the hidden knot, the rope seems quite unprepared and can be given away at the end of the trick.

A young audience particularly enjoys being taught a "trick" they can show their friends. Naturally you should not give away any real magic secrets, nor try to teach anything too difficult.

The next "bit of business" serves both to entertain your audience and to give them something their friends will find funny, too. It is a very old skit which was made famous in vaudeville, but few people have seen it today.

YOU MUST PAY THE RENT

Mysto picks up a piece of paper and offers to teach his audience a little act they can do with it.

"This is not real magic, but I'd like to show you a trick that lets one piece of paper help you pretend to be three different people."

He folds the paper back and forth until it is accordian pleated. Then he introduces the characters in his story.

First he holds the pleated paper in the middle so the two ends open out. He holds it against the side of his head so it looks like a hair bow.

"Meet Paula Purebred, our dauntless heroine."

Next he moves the paper down under his nose so it is like a moustache.

"Here's Dirty Dan, the villain man!"

Finally he moves the paper down to his collar so it looks like an old fashioned bow tie.

"And here is Danny Dogood, our hero!"

"Now," continues Mysto, "let me tell you a one-act play using our three characters. Our story happens back in the early 1900's. Paula Purebred is about to be evicted from her house on a blizzardy winter night by that dastardly fiend, Dirty Dan."

Mysto holds the paper to his head and speaks in a high-pitched girl's voice.

"Oh . . . I can't pay the rent."

Mysto moves the paper down under his nose. His voice changes to a low-pitched snarl.

"But you must pay the rent!"

Again to his hair. Girl's voice.

"But I can't pay the rent."

Paper to nose. Snarl.

"But you must pay the rent."

To hair. Girl's voice.

"But I can't pay the rent."

This argument between the heroine and the villain is carried back and forth several more times accompanied by the moving of the pleated paper and the changing of the voice. Finally, the paper is moved down to the collar and the voice becomes smooth, manly, and pleasant.

"I'll pay the rent!"

Quickly Mysto moves the paper up to his head and speaks as Paula Purebred.

"My hero."

The paper goes back under the nose. Snarl.

"Curses . . . foiled again."

Mysto then lowers the paper and smiles to indicate the play is over, or he says "The End." If the audience applauds he holds the paper back under his collar and says "thank you," then does the same holding it on his hair and under his nose.

Finally he invites the audience to try the play on their parents and friends.

How?

There is no magic here, but do not let that stop you from using this wonderful skit in your magic show. A magician is first an actor and an entertainer. This routine allows you to be both. It will offer a delightful "breather" from the more serious mysteries.

It is time now to fool the audience again. Mysto is about to do it with the kind of trick that is called, by magicians, a "Sucker" trick.

A sucker trick allows the audience to think they know how it is done . . . but . . .

WHAT COLOR ARE GHOSTS?

"What color are ghosts?" asks Mysto, picking up a large brown paper envelope.

As the audience reacts, Mysto removes a big card from the envelope showing a picture of a green-colored ghost.

"This is a ghost and you will notice that it is green. But not all ghosts are green. Let me show you," he says as he slips the card back into the envelope. He invites the audience to help him scare the ghost by shouting BOO when he counts to three.

"One, two, three," says Mysto.

"BOO," shouts the audience.

"Look what you have done," says Mysto as he pulls the card out to show that the ghost is now white. "You shouted so loudly, our green ghost became pale."

The audience is not really fooled. They saw Mysto turn the envelope around before he took the card out.

"You must really help this poor little ghost turn green again," says Mysto as he slips the card back in the envelope.

"This time, when I say three, would you take back your BOO? You can do that by shouting OOB, which is Boo backwards. One, two, three."

The audience shouts OOB (and Mysto again turns the envelope around) and when the card is removed the ghost is green again.

Naturally, by now the audience is sure that there is a card with a green ghost on the front and a white ghost on the back. Mysto doesn't pay any attention, although people are beginning to suggest this aloud. He continues with the trick . . .

"Say, that was a pretty good trick you just did."

He slips the card back into the envelope.

"Let's see you change him white again. On the count of three, just shout BOO."

The audience shouts. Mysto flips the envelope over and removes the card showing the white ghost.

"So," asks Mysto, "what color ghost do you like? I like green so let's change him back with an OOB."

He replaces the card in the envelope and counts to three. When the card is removed it is green again. The audience is wild, they are insisting on telling Mysto how he is doing the trick.

"Turn the card around," they shout.

Mysto appears to be embarrassed. He tries to put the card away.

"What do you mean?" he asks.

"The white ghost is on the back. Turn the card around," the audience answers.

"Oh, you want me to turn the card around?" says Mysto.

"Yes," shouts the delighted audience.

"Like this?" asks Mysto as he twists the card around, still keeping the back toward himself.

"No, no," screams the audience," the other way. Turn it around the other way."

"Oh, the other way," says Mysto as he twists the card back in the opposite direction but still keeps the back toward his chest, "You mean this way?"

"No, no," shouts the audience, realizing that the magician is teasing them. "Show us the back, the back!"

"The back? Oh, all right," agrees Mysto as he turns around so the audience sees his back and not the card's. "There, can you all see my back all right?"

The audience is really eager now. They are so sure they know the solution to the trick and have "caught" The Great Mysto. After all, why else would he be so reluctant to let them see the back side of the card?

Finally, however, Mysto agrees to their demands.

"Oh, you want to see the back side of the card! Well why on earth didn't you just say so? Actually, the back side of the card really won't interest you much," explains Mysto as he turns the card over.

On the back is a *cartoon picture of a person painted bright red!*

The audience is really surprised.

Mysto explains: "Actually, the back side of the card is used by ghost magicians . . . they use it when they do the trick called "What color are people!"

Then, just to fool the wise ones, Mysto rips open the big envelope to show it is empty. The white ghost has vanished for good!

How?

In slang, a "sucker" is a person that is easily cheated or fooled. This trick makes a sucker of your audience. It is carefully designed to appear very simple, easily solved, and to make the magician look very foolish. Once the audience catches on to what you are up to, they feel they are very smart . . . and you are very stupid to think you are fooling them with such a trick. The harder you try to fool them, the "wiser" they become, and the surer they are of the solution.

What really happens is that you are setting them up to be completely fooled. To do it well requires a bit of acting, timing, and being very "straight-faced."

How is the trick done? This may come as a surprise. You actually do the trick exactly the way the audience suspects . . . until the last time, then you change your method and fool them all!

You will need two cards. Make them out of white, stiff cardboard that is the same on both sides. They can be any size, but the bigger the better. They must, however, fit into a large brown paper envelope. You can make the envelope yourself, or purchase a big mailing envelope at a stationery store. Cut the flap off the mailing envelope so it is open at the top.

Prepare the two cards as follows: Draw a line one-half inch in from the edge on all sides of both cards. Paint the one-half inch edge black with a marking pen or poster paint. This black edge will help you when you must hold the two cards together so they appear as one. If one does not line up exactly, the black edges will hide this nicely.

On one card paint a bright green ghost on one side and a white ghost on the other. Be sure to use exactly the same design for each ghost and put them in the same place on each side. This is best done by drawing a ghost on another sheet of paper, cutting it out, and tracing around it.

On one side of the other card draw a cartoon picture of a person and color it bright red. Leave the other side of this card blank.

To set up the trick, lay the blank side of the person card against the white side of the ghost card and slip them into the envelope together.

To perform the trick, follow the action and patter story above and the following moves will be easy to do:

1. Remove the ghost card with only the green side toward the audience. (Leave the person card in the envelope.)

2. Replace the card in the envelope in just the same position it was before. Have the audience shout BOO. Turn the envelope around and remove the ghost card to show the white ghost.

3. Replace the card in the envelope. (Person card stays in until very end of trick, but always replace ghost card in same way as at start.)

4. Have the audience shout OOB, turn the envelope, and remove the ghost card to show the green side again.

5. Repeat this several times, changing from green to white to green. Finally, to end the trick, REMOVE BOTH CARDS TOGETHER with the green-colored ghost showing. Lay the envelope on the table and hold the card(s) with both hands.

6. Joke with your audience and, finally, turn the card around to show the red person on back.

7. Set the card(s) aside, out of sight of curious eyes and hands. Pick up the envelope and tear it open to show the audience.

You will find that once you have shown the audience they were wrong in thinking the white ghost was on the back, they will immediately try to find another explanation. Usually they will suspect the card with the white ghost is still in the envelope.

Do not be in a hurry to tear it open. Be a little reluctant. Let them think, for a moment, that they have caught you again.

When you finally do tear it open you will have succeeded in fooling them completely. They will probably have no more "explanations" . . . for fear of being made "suckers" still another time!

Children enjoy hearing a good story. It allows them to use their imaginations.

Some magic tricks can be worked into a story. Together the story and the trick make a very different kind of "act." Mysto tries to do one story trick at every party show. The following is so simple that it can always be kept ready. It also makes a nice "emergency trick" . . . one that can be done anytime another trick doesn't work.

THE STORY OF THE STRONG MAN'S BELT

"A long time ago," begins the Great Mysto, "I was a magician with the circus."

"As I was walking by the big top one day I heard a terrible argument going on."

"Someone was shouting 'it's mine,' and other voices were shouting 'it's ours.' I couldn't imagine what was going on so I went inside."

"The fat lady and the Siamese twins were having a terrible argument. Now you know who the fat lady is but have you ever seen any Siamese twins? They are two people joined together. The three of them, the fat lady and the Siamese twins, were fighting over a beautiful belt."

Mysto takes a wide loop made from newspaper from his suitcase.

"To show you what happened I will use this newspaper belt. The real belt they were fighting over had belonged to Goliath, the strong man. He had left the circus and forgotten his beautiful golden belt. The fat lady and the Siamese twins wanted the belt. They were tugging the belt so hard I was sure they would rip it, so I offered to help."

"Oh, Mighty Mysto, can you really help us?" they asked.

"Of course," I said.

"With magic?" they asked.

"No, with scissors!" I answered.

Mysto takes out a pair of scissors and cuts the paper belt down the middle to make two narrower belts.

"There," I said, handing over two belts. "Now you all have a belt."

"Thank you," said the fat lady, "but this belt is much too small for my waist."

"Thank you," said the Siamese twins, "but this belt will not fit both of us because we are hitched together."

"Can't you help us more?" they asked.

"Now, being the greatest magician in the whole world, I certainly could not let them down. So I waved my scissors over one of the belts and said the magic word 'beltgrow.' Then I cut it down the middle."

Mysto cuts the belt down the center, but when he completes the cut he does not have two more belts . . . instead he has made the one belt twice as big.

"This made a perfect size belt for the fat lady."

"Then again," he continues, "I waved my scissors over the other belt and said the magic work 'beltlink.' Then I cut this one right down the middle."

Again Mysto cuts and, upon completing the cut, discovers he has made two belts this time . . . but they are linked together.

"Aha, this made the perfect belt for the Siamese twins who were joined together just like the belt they now wear."

How?

The success of this trick depends a good deal on your being a good storyteller. Change your voice when you speak for the fat lady or the Siamese twins. Ham it up about being "the world's greatest magician." Make the story better: Give the characters names, talk more about your days with the circus, make the story fit your personality. The story is the entertainment. The trick is easy. You can make the trick in five minutes and it will just about work itself with practically no practice on your part.

The belt is actually a mathematical principle called a "Moebius Strip." It was discovered over 100 years ago by a German mathematician and astronomer called Augustus Ferdinand Moebius.

Here is how you make it: Cut a long strip of newspaper three inches wide and four feet in length. You can tape pieces together to get it long enough. With scissors, ① split the ends down about three inches in the middle.

Bring the two ends of the loop together and match up the four flaps.

Now, here is the secret:

Fasten the two flaps on the top together with sticky tape BUT, before you do, ② give the left one one-half a twist.

Fasten the flaps on the bottom together, ③ but give the left one a whole twist before you do.

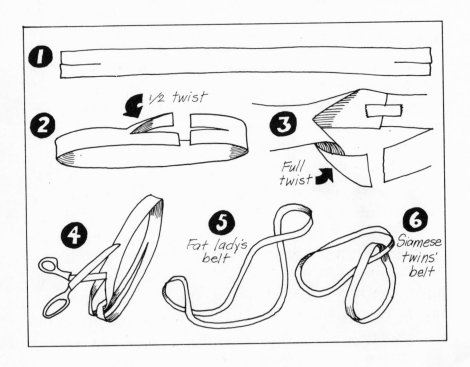

When you are done, press the belt flat so the twists don't stick out. *Keep this side with the slits and twists facing away from the audience.*

Now ④ cut right down the middle, lengthwise between the two twisted flaps. This will now produce the two belts! Unknown to the audience, one will be half-twisted, and the other will have a full twist.

Then when you cut the belt with the half twist (cut right down the middle) you will produce a single belt twice as long. Perfect for the fat lady ⑤! And by cutting the belt with the full twist (cutting down the middle) you will make two belts linked together. Ideal for Siamese twins ⑥!

Make the belt carefully and you will even amaze yourself when you cut it the first time.

Once you catch on to making the belts you can make them very quickly. Make a dozen or so and have them in your suitcase. This allows you to do the trick anytime with no more preparation.

To make the trick bigger, try inviting three people up to act as the fat lady and the twins. Let them "act" out the story and do the cutting of their belts. Give them the belts for souvenirs afterwards. Just one thing . . . be sure to invite the skinniest girl in the audience to play the part of the fat lady. This will make the audience laugh and will not embarrass the girl, as it might if you chose someone who really was worried about being too fat!

Now Mysto must wrap up his show. His final trick must be short, snappy, and in keeping with the fact that this is a party. Also, because no curtains will close when he is done, Mysto must let the audience know that he is finished with his magic. He will do this with his patter and by choosing a good ending trick.

SOMETHING IN THE NEWSPAPER

Mysto picks up a sheet of newspaper. He turns it back and forth to show both sides as he pretends to be looking for something.

"Now we come to the end of our magic show for today. Perhaps you will read all about it in the paper tomorrow. As you can see there is nothing in the paper today," he says as he continues to show the paper on both sides.

"Tomorrow, though, the paper will be different. Tomorrow you will be able to find something in the paper."

Mysto has rolled the newspaper into a tube and suddenly he breaks it in half.

"Particularly if you are a magician. A magician can always find something important in the paper."

He begins to pull out a large bright red silk.

"You look carefully in your newspaper tomorrow. Perhaps you will read how The Great Mysto stopped by today to wish Johnny Jones a very . . ."

He pulls the silk completely out, and opens it to show a big HAPPY BIRTHDAY written across it.

"Remember . . . the best news is always good news . . . and a birthday is the best news of all. So thank you for inviting me to your party, and Longfellow, my magic rabbit, and I wish you many, many more happy birthdays to come."

How?

This simple trick requires some practice but it works so well you will want to do it often once you master it.

First make a tube out of a sheet of newspaper. To make it the right size, roll it around the end of your index fingers and fasten it with paste or glue. The length of the tube should be about half the width of a sheet of newspaper. You would be wise to make several of them at the same time. You will ruin one each time you perform the trick.

Buy a large, 36 inch square, silk kerchief at the store and carefully letter the words HAPPY BIRTHDAY on it with a felt-tipped pen. Be sure to use a pen that is "water-proof" and "permanent."

When the silk is dry, roll it neatly and poke it into one of the tubes you made earlier.

To perform: Have the newspaper sheet (a single sheet only) lying in your suitcase with the loaded tube underneath. As you pick up the paper to begin the trick, slip your thumb into the tube, while your hand holds it behind the paper at the top.

Hold the paper up so the audience can see one side. With your free hand lift up the bottom of the paper and loop it away from you up into the hand holding the top. Catch it with the fingers and allow the top to fall down.

Properly done, all you do is turn the paper over so you show both sides, yet you always keep the tube hidden behind it at the top.

By repeating this simple action, you can show both sides over and over. Just lift the bottom and let the top fall down, while always holding one end in your hand with the tube.

Try doing this in front of a mirror and you will be surprised at how natural it looks. Your eye sees both sides of the paper so it seems nothing could be hidden.

To finish the trick, simply roll the sheet into a rough tube right around the tube containing the silk. Rip open the paper tubes and open it out. Chalk up another miracle . . . and another show for The Great Mysto!

CHAPTER FOUR

MYSTO THE MYSTIC

There is one thing special about most magic tricks: They are impossible! Nobody can really saw a lady in half, create a live rabbit in an empty hat, or make someone float in the air. Magicians seem to make these impossible things happen; in fact they work hard finding new impossible things they can make happen. A magician's job is to do the very things everyone knows he can't do.

A mystic's job is a bit different. A mystic does things that everyone thinks are impossible, but then everything he does might be explained by belief in supernatural powers.

If you look in a dictionary you will read that a mystic deals in things like the supernatural, the occult, palm reading, fortune telling, E.S.P., and mind reading. How about you? Do you believe in ghosts? Extra Sensory Perception? Mind reading?

A magician can be a mystic. To be one, he simply selects tricks that deal with mystical things. All of his "experiments" are magic tricks, but he chooses tricks that are not completely impossible . . . but which make you wonder if he doesn't have some special "power."

Sometimes, just for fun, Mysto likes to be a mystic. He likes to "see with his mind" and pretend to be a mentalist. A mentalist is the magician's term for a mind reader. Nobody in the world can really read minds, but there are lots of tricks mentalists can do that make audiences wonder. Mysto enjoys doing some once in awhile. You might, too!

Just one thing, please do not try to be a mystic all the time. Try an occasional mind reading show at a special party or during the Halloween season or for some adults if your parents ask you to "do a trick." This is a very special kind of magic. Small children don't understand it, older children get bored by too much of it, and only certain magicians are able to really carry it off well. Remember, you can put an occasional mind reading trick in any show you do. Try it out this way, one trick at a time, until you are able to do it well. Then you'll be ready one day to perform a whole show as "Mysto the Mystic . . . with his mysteries of the mind."

MIND SIGHT

Mysto the Mystic steps before his audience holding only a deck of cards in a case. He removes the deck and hands it to the audience requesting that it be well shuffled.

This is done, and Mysto slips the deck back into the case and folds the cover down to seal it inside. The case is then handed to a spectator.

"Would you please hold the deck over your head?" instructs Mysto.

"Now, for my first experiment, just to sharpen my mind's eye, I will attempt to look into that case and identify the bottom card on the deck."

Mysto closes his eyes and begins to concentrate.

"Ah, I am beginning to see a color . . . red. Yes, the card is a red card . . . a diamond, yes. Now let me see which diamond. Ah, a court card. A lady . . . the queen of diamonds, that's it. Would you slip the deck out and check the bottom card?"

The case is removed, by the spectator, and the bottom card is shown to be the queen of diamonds. Mysto asks that the deck be immediately returned to the case.

"Some of you may not believe that I am able to actually see with my mind. Some of you feel that I peeked at the bottom card while I was putting the deck in the box. I would like to make all of you believers. I certainly could not have glanced at the top card could I? Or the second, or third? Well let me try to see these cards, too."

Again Mysto closes his eyes and concentrates very hard on the case being held by the spectator.

"Ah yes, I see the top card very clearly. It is the three of spades . . . oh, and the next card down is the six of clubs . . . yes, the third card down is the ace of spades . . . oh, I can see the fourth card too . . . the two of diamonds! Please take the cards out now and check them."

The cards are again removed and the top four cards are checked. They are the three of spades, the six of clubs, the ace of spades, and the two of diamonds, just as Mysto said.

"In fact," Mysto continues, "now that the deck is out of the case they are even easier to see with my mind. The next card is the king of hearts and the one following the king is the five of spades."

The next two cards are flipped over. Mysto is, of course, correct.

"Now that my brain is really warmed up," says Mysto, "let's proceed to some even harder tests."

How?

This trick does not require the impossible ability to "see with your mind," but it does require some real brain work on your part. You must remember the order of six cards.

First, remove six cards from the deck and arrange them in any order you like. You will find some orders are easier to remember than others. Remember their order well . . . the whole success of the trick depends on it.

Place these six cards in the card case. Be sure they are pushed in all the way. Next, push in the rest of the deck, but do not push it completely in. Leave about half an inch of the deck sticking out. The trick is now set up and ready.

To perform, walk out holding the card case. As you do, pull the deck out of the case, secretly leaving the six arranged cards inside. This is most easily done if you hold the case in one hand with your fingers hanging over the open top to keep the six cards from sliding out with the deck. Immediately hand the deck out for a thorough shuffling.

After it is shuffled, and while you are slipping it back into the card case, catch a peek at the bottom card and remember it. Don't try too hard to be secretive about this peek, it really won't matter if anyone sees you do it.

When the deck is returned to the case, be sure it goes in so the six cards end up on top of the deck. Now, unknown to anyone, you have added six cards you know to the top of a well-shuffled deck.

The rest of the trick is acting.

Follow the description of the trick above. First, name

the bottom card. If someone suggests you peeked, appear upset. If nobody suggests you peeked . . . suggest it yourself. This is just to prepare your audience for the real "blockbuster" of naming cards down from the top. If they think you "peeked" it will throw them off from suspecting the way you really did the trick.

Finally, name the top four cards and have them checked. Immediately afterwards, name the next two cards. Do not let on that you only know six cards. Draw out your naming them and make it appear as though you could continue through the entire deck if you cared to. Remember, if you don't name the next card you will make people wonder if you could . . . and that is a mentalist's job, to create wonder.

Cards lend themselves nicely to mental magic tricks. Most everyone knows them and their pictures, symbols, and numbers can create a wide variety of effects. It is a simple matter to follow Mysto's first trick with still another card trick, one that uses real audience participation.

MEET YOUR MATCH

Mysto hands two decks of playing cards to a spectator and asks that they be thoroughly examined. The spectator is

to choose one deck for himself and hand the
o Mysto.

plains Mysto, "would you please watch me very
everything with your deck that I do with
very hard, with your copying me, it is pos-
vo minds may become tuned together so
n think alike."

ds to shuffle and cut his deck several
move he waits until the spectator, using
plicated it.

l exchange decks, just to be sure neither of
sly knows the order of any cards," Mysto

xchange decks. With his new deck, Mysto re-
and bottom cards and pokes them in the
deck. He fans the cards, picks one out, and
he spectator is following his every move.
or the helper sees the other's cards. Then
eir cards to the deck and the decks are cut.
xchange our decks one more time," suggests
her of us knows what card the other has cho-
oth know our own cards."
s are exchanged.

"Would you now look through your deck a[nd]
card you chose? I will do the same with my de[ck]
my card at the same time."

Mysto and the spectator thumb throug[h]
remove a single card each.   "Remember,
"I suggested at the start that if our hands
other's motions, it might be possible for ou[r]
too. Let me show you what I meant by
three of hearts . . .   if our minds are trul[y]
I'll bet you did, too!"

The spectator turns his card over.

It is the three of hearts.

How?

This trick is much simpler than it looks to th[e]
requires only two decks of unprepared car[ds]
borrow them, so much the better.

First with the spectator following your a[ction]
and cut the cards several times. Do this slowl[y]
he follows you very carefully. This should
very important, even though it isn't in the leas[t]

Next you must do your one bit of "dirty w[ork]
spectator is copying your last shuffle, tip the bo[ttom]

also asked to choose one deck for himself and hand the other back to Mysto.

"Now," explains Mysto, "would you please watch me very carefully and do everything with your deck that I do with mine? If we try very hard, with your copying me, it is possible that our two minds may become tuned together so that they will even think alike."

Mysto proceeds to shuffle and cut his deck several times. After each move he waits until the spectator, using his deck, has duplicated it.

"Now we will exchange decks, just to be sure neither of us subconsciously knows the order of any cards," Mysto says.

The two exchange decks. With his new deck, Mysto removes the top and bottom cards and pokes them in the center of the deck. He fans the cards, picks one out, and looks at it. The spectator is following his every move. Neither Mysto or the helper sees the other's cards. Then they return their cards to the deck and the decks are cut.

"Let us exchange our decks one more time," suggests Mysto. "Neither of us knows what card the other has chosen, but we both know our own cards."

The decks are exchanged.

"Would you now look through your deck and find the card you chose? I will do the same with my deck and find my card at the same time."

Mysto and the spectator thumb through their decks and remove a single card each.   "Remember," explains Mysto, "I suggested at the start that if our hands duplicated each other's motions, it might be possible for our minds to do so, too. Let me show you what I meant by this. I chose the three of hearts . . . if our minds are truly tuned together, I'll bet you did, too!"

The spectator turns his card over.

It is the three of hearts.

How?

This trick is much simpler than it looks to the audience. It requires only two decks of unprepared cards. If you can borrow them, so much the better.

First with the spectator following your actions, shuffle and cut the cards several times. Do this slowly and be sure he follows you very carefully. This should appear to be very important, even though it isn't in the least!

Next you must do your one bit of "dirty work." As the spectator is copying your last shuffle, tip the bottom of your deck up a bit, pull back the very bottom card with your thumb, and glance at the second card in from the bottom. Remember this *second* card. It is your "key" card.

Now exchange decks with the spectator. Remove the top card and, without looking at it, poke it anywhere into the deck. Wait until your helper does this also.

Then remove the bottom card, facedown, and push it anywhere into the middle of the deck. Wait until your helper does this with his deck.

(If you're following carefully, you now know that your "key" card is on the bottom of the deck the spectator holds.)

Fan out your cards and pull one out. Do not allow anyone to see it. Look at it, and lay it facedown on the squared up deck. Have your helper do the same with his deck, but caution him not to allow you to see the card. (Note: it is not necessary, really, for you to remember the card you picked out . . . read on and you will understand why.)

Cut the deck one time. This is the trick. As your helper cuts his deck he puts the bottom card (the "key" card) on top of the card he has selected, remembered, and put on top of the deck.

Now you exchange decks once again.

Ask him to look through his deck and find his card and you will do the same with your deck. Actually he will be looking through your deck for the card he picked, and at the same time you, too, will be looking through his deck for the card he selected. To find the card all you must do is find the "key" card and remove the card right in front of it.

All that remains is for you to claim that this card was the one you selected originally (a little magician's fib) and . . . surprise . . . it will match the one the spectator found in the other deck!

Naturally, the trick is so simple to do and so surprising to an audience, there is a great temptation to do it over and over. Don't do it. Remember, as a mentalist you must always leave people wondering if it happened because of "chance." By repeating the same thing again and again, you are just proving that you can do a very clever trick, and your mental mystery becomes just a puzzling magical exercise.

Do not overdo card tricks. Some people do not like them; some get bored easily by them. Worse, many people will begin to suspect that they are "trick cards" and that you need them to do your "mind reading." Prove that you are really Mysto the Mystic by using other things, too.

MYSTO THE POSTMAN

Mysto invites a spectator to help him. He waits onstage for a minute while Mysto goes into the audience. Down in the audience Mysto hands five envelopes, all exactly alike, to five people at random. Then he returns to the stage.

"Some people say that objects that belong to a person atune themselves to that person and will send out waves that identify their owner. If this puzzles you, let's try an experiment to see if and how it happens. I have distributed five envelopes and I will now turn my back. Would the people holding the envelopes drop in any small personal object . . . such as a pencil, comb, coin, or anything you might have . . . and seal the envelope."

This is done.

"My assistant here will now collect the envelopes and mix them thoroughly. Then he will tell me to face you again."

When this is done, Mysto turns and faces the audience. He asks for the envelopes.

Carefully Mysto studies each envelope. He places them one by one against his forehead and he mumbles loudly. Suddenly he looks at the audience.

"I feel I can identify each object now, and I know who owns it. Please see if I am correct."

Quickly Mysto rushes down into the audience. He hands each of the five spectators an envelope and asks them to open it.

Back up on the stage, Mysto asks each of the spectators in turn if he was correct in returning that particular envelope to them. They all agree.

Mysto the Mystic has somehow succeeded in returning the five correct items to the five correct spectators.

How?

There is a very clever "trick" within this trick. Probably you were fooled by just reading the description. If you were, you can be sure your whole audience will be, too. You probably think the trick is knowing what the objects are. But it isn't!

All you really need to remember, is which envelope you give to which spectator. The envelopes are important . . . not what goes in them.

Take five envelopes and prepare them in the following way:

Envelope # 1   do nothing to it.

Envelope # 2   fold down the upper left corner.

Envelope # 3   fold down the upper right corner.

Envelope # 4   fold down the lower left corner.

Envelope # 5   fold down the lower right corner.

Straighten out all the folds so the envelopes look flat and normal, but so that you can still see where the creases were made. You must first remember which envelope represents which number. Have them stacked one through five. During the trick, you go into the audience and hand out the envelopes. You must do this yourself, so that you can later remember which spectator received which envelope.

When you return to the stage and turn your back, have the objects sealed inside and then have them collected and shuffled by your helper on stage. (This helper, by the way, must be a spectator so nobody will suspect he gives you any clues.)

When you have the envelopes in your hands, you must then become an actor. Puzzle over them. Mumble, concentrate, look at the audience, appear worried. Take your time. Pretend this is a very difficult task.

At the same time, find the creases and stack the envelopes one through five. Finally walk back into the audience and hand the envelopes back. Do it quickly and do not give them back in order, but move around passing them here and there.

Ask that they be opened and checked. Naturally, you will have given the correct objects to the correct spectators. Really though, all you have done is passed out five envelopes, collected them, and returned them to the same five spectators. You will get credit, however, for doing a far greater trick. Let people think you are a great mind reader. Don't tell them that you are simply a postman delivering "addressed" envelopes to the correct "addresses" without having any idea about the "letters" inside!

Up until now Mysto has been quite serious in trying to prove that he is a "mystic." This can get boring to an audience. It is good to include a bit of humor, even in a mind reading act.

PHOOEY . . .

Inviting a spectator up to help him with an experiment, Mysto stares hard at his face then he picks up a pad of paper and a pencil.

"I am going to try a very hard kind of mind reading. Instead of telling you what you are thinking about right now I am going to tell you what you are going to be thinking in the future."

Quickly Mysto writes a message on the pad and tears off

the sheet. He folds it in quarters and hands it to another member of the audience for safekeeping.

"Now let me try an experiment with you." Mysto picks up two small envelopes off the table and holds one in each hand. "Would you please point to either of these en-velopes."

The spectator chooses one.

"Would you care to change your mind?" teases Mysto. "You can if you like, but you must do it now. Of course, you are perfectly free to keep the one you have already selected."

The spectator makes his final choice. Mysto tears off the top and hands the opened envelope to the helper.

"Would you please examine the contents of the en-velope you have chosen."

The helper spills out a folded piece of newspaper.

"Gee, that really is a shame," says Mysto as he tears off the top of the other envelope and spills out its contents. "You had an absolute free choice of either envelope and you chose the one with the piece of newspaper. Now, if you had only chosen this one," he says as he opens the other envelope and pulls out a dollar bill, "you would have been richer by a dollar."

The audience is a bit surprised; the helper is a bit disappointed. Mysto turns immediately to the person still holding the folded prediction slip.

"Remember when I promised to write your thoughts before you even knew what they would be?" says Mysto as he takes the slip and hands it to his helper. "Would you read my prediction please?"

The spectator opens the slip and reads it aloud: PHOOEY.

"And that," announces Mysto, "is exactly what you thought when you got the newspaper instead of the dollar bill, isn't it?"

How?

First you must ham it up a bit and finally write your prediction of what your helper will think. Naturally, you simply write PHOOEY. The trick is not the prediction—that is just for a final laugh. The trick is to have the person always select the newspaper and never the dollar bill.

How can you honestly give him a free choice in choosing an envelope and still be sure he does not choose the bill? You really can do it. All you need is two envelopes . . . and two pieces of newspaper and two one-dollar bills!

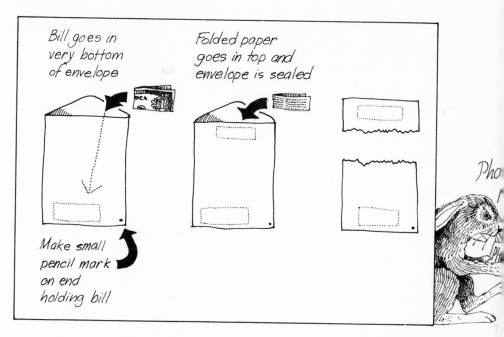

Bill goes in very bottom of envelope

Folded paper goes in top and envelope is sealed

Make small pencil mark on end holding bill

Fold the bills and the bill-sized newspaper strips into very small bundles. Push a bill into one end of each envelope. If you use the small manila "pay" envelopes from a stationery store it will work much better. Then place the folded paper in the opposite end and seal each envelope.

With a pencil make a small dot on the end of each envelope where the bill is located. Lay them on your table, and you are ready for the trick.

Hold the envelopes, one in each hand, and offer your helper his free choice of either. As you hold them up, squeeze the envelopes in the middle so the newspaper and bill stay at opposite ends.

Let your helper change his mind as often as he likes. It really doesn't matter, because both envelopes contain exactly the same things at the moment.

When your helper finally chooses, hold the selected envelope with the pencil dot up. Tear off the end, with the bill hidden inside. Hand the bottom of the envelope to him to open. Naturally, he will have only the envelope containing a folded strip of newspaper. As he looks, casually drop the top end of the envelope (with the hidden bill) into your pocket.

When you tear open your envelope, do it the same way . . . except be sure to hold it bill end down, so you will tear off the end with the newspaper strip hidden inside.

Easy? It almost sounds too easy to fool anyone, but it really does. Your audience might assume your helper's selection was entirely by luck . . . later, though, your "prediction" of PHOOEY will remind them that you really did know beforehand what was going to happen. Then, your comedy trick starts to become a genuine mystery!

If you would like to take a real breather from the mystery, you might enjoy trying a simple bit of business that suggests something mysterious, but turns into just a cute trick everyone is let in on.

I'M GOING TO MAKE A GHOST APPEAR

"I'm going to make a ghost appear. In fact, I'm going to teach everyone in this audience how to make a ghost appear," says Mysto. He then begins his trick by inviting a young lady up to assist him.

"I am going to teach everyone how to make a ghost appear . . . except you! You, my dear young lady, have been chosen instead to actually feel the touch of a real live ghost."

Mysto turns the girl to one side so he is facing her and the audience can see them both from the side. He holds his hands with the pointing fingers held straight up and his other fingers curled into fists. The back of the hands are toward Mysto himself.

"To make this ghost appear we will hold a short seance," Mysto says. "A seance must be held in the dark. One reason for holding them in the dark is so nobody can see if any trickery is being used. For this very reason our lady assistant will be in the dark, but all of you will be allowed to remain in the light. I will ask her to close her eyes, and I will rest one finger on each of her eyelids so she will always know where my hands are."

Mysto places a fingertip *very gently* on each eyelid.

"Now you can feel my fingertips so you know exactly where my hands are and, with my fingertips on your eyelids, I know you are completely in the dark. Now let's try to conjure up a ghost. Ah, yes, I believe I see one floating in the room right now . . . right over your head. Audience, can you all see the ghost?"

The audience shouts, "Yes."

"And he is coming closer and closer to the girl."

Again the audience shouts, "Yes."

"Watch it, I think the ghost is going to actually touch you. If it does, will you please scream so we know it," Mysto says.

Suddenly the girl feels a ghostly touch running through her hair and down across her face. She screams.

"Now," explains Mysto, "I can see the ghost vanishing again into a cloud of ectoplasm . . . gone!"

He removes his fingers from the girl's eyes, which she immediately opens. She and Mysto are alone on the stage.

"Please," asks Mysto, talking to the audience, "please do not tell her where the ghost has gone, but let her forever wonder if she was indeed touched by a real ghost here today. Remember that many, many of the ghosts we have heard about have been conjured up in much the same way and, now that you all know the secret, please feel free to conjure up a ghost the same way anytime you like."

Mysto winks at the audience!

How?

Everyone loves to be let in on a magic secret. This trick lets you share a simple secret with your entire audience. And you can be sure that someone will tell the girl what actually happened. The fun is thinking about it and, later, trying it on friends at home. It is really an uncanny feeling. Even when you know how it works it feels strange when someone tries it on you.

Follow the patter story above. When your helper is selected and facing you, hold up your two pointing fingers so she can see them. Point them toward her eyes. Naturally, she will not wish for you to poke her in the eyes, so she will automatically shut them. If she doesn't, just ask her to shut her eyes when your fingertips are almost touching her eyelids. When your fingertips rest on her eyelids she thinks that she really knows where your hands are . . . but, she is wrong!

As your forefingers approach her eyes, and just after they close, simply spread the first two fingers on one of your hands out like a "Y" and let one finger rest on each eyelid. This will leave your other hand completely free, and yet she feels a finger on each lid and assumes you are using both hands.

Now, with your free hand, you can brush her hair lightly, touch her face, run a "ghostly" finger down her arm, or whatever.

Be sure to ask the audience if they can see the ghost. They will quickly "catch on" and, if you smile and wink at them, will go along with your trick.

When you are finally ready to have the girl open her eyes, just move your free hand back to her face and point the index finger right toward her eye. As you remove your other hand from her eyelids, fold the one extra finger back. As her eyes open she will see two fingers—one on each hand which is the same thing she saw just before her eyes closed.

The audience will enjoy the little joke you played. The girl will be thoroughly confused by it. You can be sure she will later pester her friends until they let her in on how it was done. This is fine because all you really wanted to do was entertain your audience and teach them a very simple trick.

If you are asked to do a show for a small group of people, you can often find tricks that work best in that situation. Many of these will not work anywhere else. The next trick is a perfect example.

HAIRPIN HYPNOTISM

Mysto places a table knife and a small piece of wire bent into a "U" shape on a table and asks the audience, "Do you believe in hypnotism?"

He then asks a spectator to help him. He hands him the table knife and asks that it be held parallel to the tabletop and a few inches above it.

"I am now going to place this bent wire on the knife, like a cowboy riding his horse. In fact, that is exactly what I want you to think of—a horse and a rider."

"Now I am going to ask you to lower the knife until the

"rider's" feet just touch the tabletop. Your job will be to try to keep the rider in his saddle and not let him ride down the knife. My job will be to hypnotize you so you cannot stop him!"

The spectator lowers the knife until the ends of the wire horseshoe just touch the tabletop. Just as this happens, Mysto says:

"Look out now he is beginning to ride. He is starting to ride down the knife. Keep his feet touching . . . you can't stop him . . . there he goes . . ."

The wire slides down the knife in a series of tiny hops. No matter how hard the spectator tries to stop the rider by holding his hand still, Mysto always seems to be able to make the wire hop along the blade.

Other spectators think that the first spectator is not really trying hard. Mysto invites anyone to try. Everyone who does also fails. The tiny bent wire skips mysteriously down the knife blade, apparently at Mysto's command, no matter how hard the spectator tries to prevent it.

How?

Surprisingly there is no hypnotism, or even any magic, here. This is actually an old, but seldom seen, science "trick."

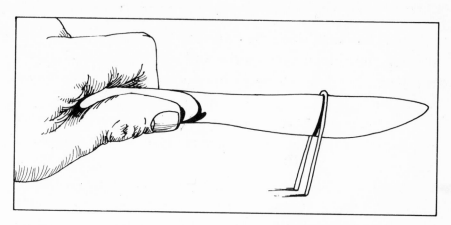

Our muscles are in constant motion. They keep our arms, legs, and bodies in position. We cannot always feel or see our muscles moving but they are moving back and forth constantly to keep our bodies exactly where we want them. These tiny muscle movements make this trick work by itself!

Try it on yourself right now. Hold a table knife over a tabletop with the cutting edge up. Be sure to use a dull-edged knife so there can be no accidents. Make a wire horeshoe with both "legs" of equal length out of a piece of wire or a paper clip. Loop the wire over the middle of the knife blade. Slowly lower the blade until the two ends of the wire just touch the tabletop. Keep the tips of the wire lightly touching the tabletop and the wire rider will begin to hop down the blade. You cannot stop this from happening no matter how hard you try, unless you lift the wire off the tabletop (which is "cheating"). Your arm and hand muscles are trying to keep your hand still. To do this they must constantly tug back and forth. You can't see or feel the tugging, but that delicate shaking is what shakes the wire along the blade.

When you have done it yourself, you will know exactly how to tell your spectators to do the same thing. Now all you have to be is a bit of an actor and convince your friends that it is your ability as a hypnotist that permits you to have this strange control over them.

One last thing, if people try it themselves later, they will discover they still can't do it even though you are not there to "hypnotize" them. Therefore, you might end by saying, "Even if you try this later, it will still be impossible for you to keep the rider on the knife. Now that I have given you my hypnotic suggestion, it will remain with you forever. If you don't believe it . . . try this experiment any time you like at any time in the future . . . you will never be able to do it from this day on!"

Whenever possible use up-to-date ideas in any kind of magic show. Perhaps you cannot duplicate the marvels of science such as space travel, growing plants without soil, or television . . . then again, perhaps with a little acting you can appear to do even more unbelievable things. Mysto, and you, should always try to up-date tricks to make them understandable and modern. The next effect will give you a good example.

THE AMAZING PICTURE TRANSMISSION

"Television," explains Mysto, "is a wonderful way of sending pictures invisibly from one place to another. Some people are puzzled by its mystery, but we magicians have been doing similar things for years. Let me demonstrate."

Mysto invites two helpers up from the audience. He places them about ten feet apart, one on each side of him.

"You will be the sender," he says to the first helper. "And you will be the receiver," he says to the second.

Mysto picks up a pad of paper and tears off the top blank sheet. He folds the paper several times and hands it to the receiver.

"You will be a receiver just like our home television set. It will be your job to catch the signals from the television station that is transmitting the picture. Your 'screen' will be this blank sheet of paper. Hold it up high so we can all watch it."

Mysto then crosses over to the other helper. He holds the pad so everyone can see the top sheet and he begins to draw a simple picture with a dark crayon.

"You will be the T.V. station, the sender. It will be your job to transmit this picture to that receiver over there," Mysto gestures to the helper on the other side of the stage.

Mysto has finished his drawing. He holds the picture up so the audience can see it; then he tears off the sheet and folds it several times. He hands the folded sheet to the sender and sets the pad aside.

"Now," explains Mysto, "our sender has a picture he would like to transmit to the receiver. Would you like to see the picture travel visibly, so you can see it go, or invisibly, so you can't?"

"Visibly!" shouts the audience.

"Okay," says Mysto as he takes the paper from the sender and begins to walk toward the receiver with it. "This is how we do it visibly!"

"In fact," he continues, "Some pictures are transmitted visibly like this . . . but we don't call it television . . . we call it the United States mail! Now, wouldn't you really like to see it go invisibly?"

"Yes," says the audience, realizing that Mysto has been pulling their legs.

He returns the folded paper to the sender and asks him to concentrate very hard on the picture. He is to "imagine the picture flying through the air and landing on the paper held by the receiver."

Walking to the receiver, Mysto asks him to concentrate on catching a picture on his paper. Suddenly Mysto stops. . .

"Oh, no!" gasps Mysto. "You don't even have your antenna up. Please hold your hand like this." And he shows the helper how to hold two fingers of his free hand up like a "V" on top of his head.

"Good, good. Now your 'rabbit ears' are in place and you should be receiving a clear signal. Are you?"

As the helper begins to look puzzled, or answers "no," Mysto says in a loud whisper that everyone can hear, "Say YES."

"Good," shouts Mysto, "There is no channel interference or technical difficulty. Our transmission is coming through loud and clear."

Turning to the sender, he asks, "Are you all through with your transmission?"

As the sender starts to answer, Mysto again whispers loudly, "Say YES."

"Then you no longer have the picture at your studio?" questions Mysto. "Will you open your paper and see."

The sender opens his folded paper and finds that it is now completely blank!

"Would you now say," Mysto continues, "that it would be a fine mystery if our receiver has actually caught that same picture on his piece of paper?"

Remembering that the receiver is still holding the folded sheet of blank paper that Mysto gave him at the very beginning . . . and has not been near since . . . the audience agrees that it would indeed be impossible.

"Now then," Mysto addresses the receiver, "open your paper and show the audience if you really did receive anything."

The paper is opened and the picture is there, just as it was originally drawn on the other sheet.

"A lot of people have dreams about being a star on television. These two helpers have done far better than that . . . they have proven that they *are* televisions—one was a whole set, and the other was a whole station. Now what T.V. star do you know who can make that claim?"

Mysto sends his helpers back to their chairs, allowing them to keep their papers to study and puzzle over later.

How?

This trick works very simply, but it will require some nerve on your part to carry it off. In spite of your "modern day" talk about T.V. the basic idea is a very old one. Years ago magicians did similar tricks while referring to ghosts, spirits, or invisible assistants.

You will need a pad of paper and a little preparation. The only other prop you will require is a dark crayon or felt-tip marking pen. The pad should be plain white, without lines. The larger it is, the better.

Cut off an inch from the bottom of the top sheet on the pad. Lift the shortened top sheet and draw a large simple picture on the second sheet. Make it a drawing of a star or an easy cartoon face that you can duplicate later.

If you are not a good artist, carefully trace the drawing with a *very faint pencil line* onto the top sheet. It is important that the drawing not show through when the top sheet covers it, so you may have to hold the sheets up against a bright window to do the tracing.

The pad is now completely prepared, and no further "gimmicks" are required. Now you must use your nerve . . . plus a little practice, of course!

Choose a sender and receiver and place them on each side of you (for practice, just use two tables). Pick up the pad and turn the top of it casually toward the audience to show them it is blank. Because the top of the pad is blank, your audience will just assume the pad is ordinary and empty.

Now, and this is what you must practice, turn the pad toward you and tear off the "top" sheet. *Not really* . . . what you really do is tear off the sheet by first grasping it from the bottom. Because the top sheet has been cut short, you actually tear off the sheet underneath . . . the one with the picture already drawn on it! If you do this easily and quickly it will be a perfect illusion. Everyone will be sure you have simply torn off the top sheet.

Lay the pad down. All sheets are now blank, but the top sheet is still the short one. Fold up the sheet you removed. Be careful! The audience assumes it is blank but it contains the picture you wish to keep secret at the moment. Hand it to the receiver and ask him to hold it high so everyone can see it. Be sure you never get near it again. This will make the final mystery even harder to explain.

Now pick up the pad again and walk toward the sender. Hold the pad so it faces the audience and sketch a duplicate picture on the top (short) sheet. If you traced the picture lightly in pencil lines you can simply darken it with your crayon.

When the sketch is finished, hold it up for a moment to show the audience; then turn it toward yourself, just as before. With the pad facing you, tear off the top sheet. *Not really!* Again, tear off the sheet from the bottom. Because the top sheet with the picture is short, you actually grasp the second sheet (blank) and tear that out. Again, if done naturally, your audience will assume you have removed the top sheet with the picture.

Lay the pad on the table. You must be careful when you do this because the picture is now on top. Be sure to keep the side with the picture away from the audience and lay the pad, picture down, on the table. Then fold up the sheet you removed and hand it to the sender.

The trick is done . . . from your side. To the audience, the trick is just about to begin. Thanks to your nerve and trickery you have made a double exchange: a picture for a blank sheet and a blank sheet for a picture! Now you require only a little showmanship to make this into an unbelievable mystery.

You can now let the helpers open their own papers without getting near them, and you can let them keep the papers as souvenirs. People will study these papers later, looking for "vanishing ink" or some similar trick. Probably no one will think of your real "assistant"—the pad of paper—but be sure to get it away from prying eyes as soon as possible after the conclusion of the trick.

Also emphasize the fact that you have not been near the papers since they were given to your helpers. This will make the mystery much harder for your audience to explain. Remember, even though you did touch the papers when you gave them out, nobody really thinks you began your trick until your helpers held their papers and you asked them to begin concentrating on the wonderful picture transmission!

Some "mind reading" tricks require the assistance of a confederate, or a helper. The following is a fine example. It makes a swell ending trick because it can be continued . . . particularly at a party . . . . for as long as people find it interesting. Even when people are sure your confederate is "sending" you a secret "code," it is practically impossible for them to discover what it is.

WITHOUT A WORD BEING SAID

Mysto introduces his assistant and offers to do a trick which will prove the existence of mental telepathy. He lays ten cards, the ace through the ten, on the table.

"I would like to conduct this entire experiment in silence . . . without a word being said!" Mysto explains. "I will leave the room, and while I am gone, I would like someone to point to any one of these cards. When I return, my assistant will tap each of the cards one time while I concentrate. As he taps each card, I will attempt to read his mind and he will attempt to transmit the card to me. I will then point to the card I think was selected."

"If I am correct, will the person who chose the card please nod his head? Then I will leave and we will try it again. But from this moment on, I ask that we conduct this entire experiment in silence."

Mysto leaves the room. A spectator points to one of the cards. Mysto returns. His assistant, without even looking at him, taps each card one time in turn.

When the tapping is completed, Mysto thinks for a moment, and then points to one of the cards. The spectator nods "yes."

Mysto leaves the room. The performance takes place again. Each time Mysto is able to point to the correct card. After a few trips the audience is certain that the assistant is secretly "telling" Mysto which card was selected. They watch him very carefully.

No matter how hard they watch, the assistant always does exactly the same thing in exactly the same way. There are no clues as to how he might be "communicating."

The trick is repeated many times. Finally, when Mysto is convinced his audience is thoroughly puzzled, he finishes the trick with a suggestion:

"I have really tricked you here. Now I will explain exactly how I am able to do this. I told you I was able to do it by reading my assistant's mind and he told me the correct card by mental telepathy. This, of course, was silly . . . but it sounds good. If you really want to know how it works let me explain."

The audience is eager to learn the solution to this puzzle.

"Actually, as my assistant tapped each card, I simply read your minds. When the correct card was tapped each time, every one of you said 'that's it' in your mind . . . didn't you? I thank you for doing this, because it made my job very, very easy. In fact without *your* help I would never have been able to do this trick."

How?

This trick is very simple and almost foolproof. It will require just about five minutes of your time to practice in private with your assistant. It is even possible to "pick up" an assistant at a party and teach him the trick in a back room . . . then swear him to secrecy!

Lay the ten cards on the table as shown in the illustration. The suits are not important, but be sure you have

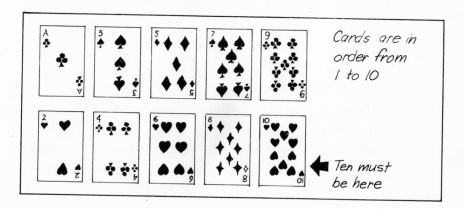

numbers one through ten (the ace is one). The ten card is the "key" to the trick. It has ten spots on it and there are ten cards on the table. Whichever card is selected, it is represented by a spot on this card. Each pip (spot) on the card will represent one of the cards. You and your assistant can decide how to "number" the pips, but here is an example:

You watch your assistant as he taps. You must look interested with every tap, but it is really the final tap . . . on the ten card . . . that tells you something. Whichever spot he taps on the ten card will immediately tell you which of the cards was selected.

If your assistant does his job well, nobody will ever notice this signal to you. They will watch for a clue when the selected card is tapped, or perhaps for some facial expression that tips you off. He can tap the cards in all different places . . . it's only the ten card that he must tap exactly right.

Even if you never present an entire act of mental magic, it is fun to include one or two in your regular show once in awhile. You will also find this kind of trick fun to do, all by itself, at a party or when someone says "show me a trick." Remember, this kind of magic does not always seem as impossible as cutting ladies in half or making elephants disappear, but it really makes your audience wonder . . . and *wonder* is a "magic word" that every magician learns to use.

CHAPTER FIVE

MYSTO GOES TO SCHOOL

The mighty Mysto has received an invitation from his teacher. It seems that she has heard that he does magic tricks and she thinks the class would enjoy seeing some.

Mysto is worried. Doing a show for kids he doesn't know well is one thing, but for his very own classmates . . . that is something else.

At first he does not want to do the show, but his teacher urges him and his classmates seem anxious that he do it. He agrees, and a day is set. Now he must go home and plan the show.

Mysto realizes that he cannot do anything that appears too serious. His classmates do not look upon him as Mr. Mysterious. To them Mysto is just another kid. He knows they like to laugh and have fun, so he will plan to do some funny things.

Mysto begins to think about a special kind of show magicians refer to as a "theme" show. Rather than just present a collection of odd tricks as he might at a birthday party, Mysto tries to use tricks that have something to do with school or he uses things that would be found around a classroom.

He considers where he will be doing the show and wonders how he can take advantage of it. He decides to use the blackboard. He knows his audience will be seated in front of him, so he can use tricks with things hidden in back. And he does not have children of different ages in the audience.

Mysto must solve some problems: he must keep his tricks quite simple, he must be ready to go during the school day, and he must carry his tricks—along with his books—to school with him. After the show he must be ready for the questions and prying eyes that will follow him the rest of the day.

A show in a classroom is quite different from almost any other kind of show. It is a challenge, and Mysto looks forward to it.

For an opening trick, he uses the blackboard and a piece of chalk. This sets the mood for his classroom magic show.

THE GRATE MYSTO

The show is on! The teacher has just introduced The Great Mysto and he walks to the blackboard with a piece of chalk. He turns, faces the board, and without saying anything, begins to write on it.

"It's too bad that our teacher is not a magician," he begins. "If she were, she could use a bit of magic to help us learn better."

Mysto's writing on the blackboard is very faint and almost impossible to read.

"If Mrs. Dexter would only write with my magic chalk, we would all be able to read her writing much better. Just watch and you will see what I mean."

Mysto starts to introduce his first real trick and, as the class watches the blackboard, the writing gradually becomes clearer and whiter. It reads:

THE GRATE MYSTO
WORLD'S GREATEZT MAGICAN
(And poorst speler)

How?

There is no real magic trick here. This is only meant to be an "attention grabbing" opener that appeals to your audience. It is different from what the teacher writes on the blackboard so it is entertaining to watch.

You will have to obtain a stick of chalk the day before your show. Place the chalk in a dish of water so it is completely covered and let it soak for a couple of hours. When it is thoroughly soaked, wipe it off and wrap it in a small piece of aluminum foil or waxed paper. The next day drop it in your pocket. Be sure the foil or waxed paper is loose so you can slip it out easily, but keep the wrapping on until the last minute. The wrapping keeps the chalk damp.

As you are being introduced, reach into your pocket and unwrap the chalk. Take it out as you step forward. Go right to the blackboard and pretend to take the chalk out of the chalk tray. Write on the board with the wet chalk. Your letters will be faint and probably unreadable. They will look very strange to the class.

Turn away from the board when you are through writing. Keep talking and perhaps prepare for your next trick, but do not really do anything that will distract attention from the blackboard. The water will begin to evaporate from the chalk and the letters will grow much whiter. They will appear very bright and outstanding. Although, at the end, they will be no whiter than letters written with dry chalk, they will appear to be so because they were so dull in the beginning. Try it yourself before you use it in a school show. It will even surprise you!

While waiting for the letters to become white, you might invite one of your classmates up to assist you with a trick. You can take a bit of time explaining what he is to do.

ANSWER "YES"

Mysto has invited a helper up to assist him. He explains that one sure thing about school is tests or examinations. He offers to play a little quiz game with his helper. If the helper can answer every question Mysto asks with the word "yes," Mysto promises to "give him a quarter."

The game begins.

"Are you glad you are up here with me?"

"Yes."

"Would you rather be home studying your homework? Or, would you rather be here making eyes at Mrs. Dexter?"

"Yes."

"Oh . . . and tell me, what is your name?"

"Yes."

"My, my, what a very strange name. Do all your friends call you Yes, too?"

"Yes."

"I suppose they would have to. They couldn't call you anything else, could they?"

"Yes."

"Oh, what else could they call you?"

"Yes."

"Well, tell me, Yes, are you a boy or a girl?"

"Yes."

"What does that mean . . . are you a boy?"

"Yes."

"Or, are you a girl?"

"Yes."

"Gee, you really are mixed up, aren't you?"

"Yes."

"Would you rather I asked you something else?"

"Yes."

"Okay, are you married?"

"Yes."

"And what is your wife's name?"

"Yes."

"Oh, Mrs. Yes . . . I guess that makes sense, doesn't it?"

"Yes."

"Oh, all right, let's get down to serious business. Tell me, do you believe in bananas?"

"Yes."

"Good, here is one."

Mysto hands the helper a banana and continues with the questions, "Do you believe in ghosts?"

"Yes."

"Do you believe a ghost can help us with a magic trick?"

"Yes."

"Do you know a ghost who can help us?"

"Yes."

"Will you call him here right now?"

"Yes."

"Have you called him?"

"Yes."

"Good. You are very cooperative. Will your ghost friend help the world's greatest magician do a trick with your banana?"

"Yes."

"You know who the world's greatest magician is, don't you?"

"Yes."

"Will you tell me his name?"

"Yes."

"What is it?"

"Yes."

"No, no. You are not a magician. Won't you tell everyone here that I, The Great Mysto, am the greatest magician in the entire world?"

"Yes."

"You wouldn't tell a lie would you?"

"Yes."

"Do you always tell the truth?"

"Yes."

"My goodness, you are very confusing. Let's have your ghost friend do his banana trick. Okay?"

"Yes."

"Can you make him cut the banana into pieces while it is still in the skin?"

"Yes."

"Boy, I'd like to see that. Are you sure he can do it?"

"Yes."

"Can you make him cut it into five hundred and fifty-three pieces?"

"Yes."

"Now let me get this straight. You are going to ask your invisible ghost friend to cut that banana you're holding into five hundred and fifty-three pieces while it is still inside its skin. Is that right?"

"Yes."

"It sounds like an awfully hard trick. Would you rather try something easier?"

"Yes."

"Okay, how about having him cut it into . . . hmm . . . four pieces while it's inside the skin."

"Yes.

"Will he do it if I count to four?"

"Yes."

"One, two, three, four. Is it done?"

"Yes."

"You mean that there are now four pieces of banana inside that skin that has never been opened?"

"Yes."

"Oh, that's impossible. I'll tell you what, do you remember that I offered you a quarter for this quiz if you answered every question with a 'yes'?"

"Yes."

"Well . . . can I change my mind now?"

"Yes."

"I've decided that if you can really do this trick with the banana I will double my offer and give you two quarters. Is that a deal?"

"Yes."

"All right. Peel the banana and let's see."

The helper peels the skin away and inside finds the banana neatly cut into four pieces. Mysto is surprised, but only for a moment.

"My goodness, you are a better magician than I am. Your ghost friend has indeed cut the banana into four pieces without even opening it. He has, it seems, cut it into four quarters . . . and I am happy to pay you off with two of the quarters."

Mysto hands his helper two pieces of the banana, and thanks him for his assistance.

How?

This is not so much of a trick as it is a short humorous routine. A routine is an "act" where one action follows another in a logical way. This kind of routine is worth working on and adding to your program.

This routine is very funny. You and your helper really work together for the laughs. You will do all the memorizing and the work, but often your helper will get the biggest laughs when he is made to answer "yes." Learn it well and add a few "choice" questions of your own if you like.

The only real trick here is how the banana gets cut into four pieces while it is still in the skin. This is a very old magic trick, and yet it is unknown to most people.

Take a long sewing needle with a length of thread attached. Push it into the banana, in one side and along the inside of the skin. Pull the needle out, then push it back into the *same* hole and "sew" the banana along the inside of the skin, then out again. As you continue sewing you will

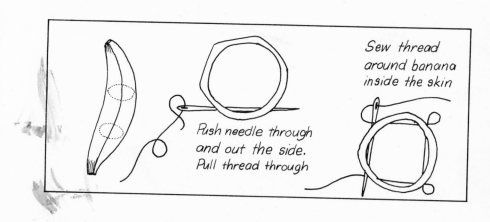

Push needle through and out the side. Pull thread through

Sew thread around banana inside the skin

make a loop of thread all around the banana inside the skin. Finally your thread will come out the *same* hole it started at. The illustrations make this very easy to understand.

Finally, pull *both* ends of the thread at the same time. This will cut the banana and remove the thread without opening the skin.

Repeat this method of cutting with thread three times in the banana and you will actually cut it into four pieces while it is inside the skin. When the banana is peeled later it will fall into four quarters without any clue as to how it happened.

Prepare the banana only a short time before you plan to use it. Perhaps you can remove it from your lunch bag for the trick. It requires only a few minutes of preparation before you leave for school in the morning.

Naturally, this trick can be done in any show. If you learn the routine well, it may easily become your favorite trick.

It would probably be a good idea to follow up this funny trick with one just a bit more serious. A "blackboard mystery" would serve to convince your classmates that you do indeed know some magic secrets.

THE TIME THAT TELLS

Walking to the blackboard, Mysto draws a big circle with a piece of chalk. He then writes the numbers one through twelve, just as they appear on a clockface.

"Can you tell me what is always covering its face with its hands?" he asks just before he writes the numbers.

"Yes, it is a clock," he says as he writes.

"Let me show you something about a clock that you will never learn in school. You were taught how to tell time, but a clock can tell you more than that."

He invites a spectator up to assist him and says, "Please think of any number you like on this clockface, but do not say it aloud."

Mysto places his hand on one of the numbers on the clock and continues, "Every time I tap one of the numbers on this clock, please add a 'one' to the number you are thinking of. Then, when you reach the number 20, please say STOP."

Mysto begins tapping. After a few numbers the helper shouts STOP.

"What number did you think of originally?" asks the magician.

"Four," responds the helper.

"Look," cries Mysto. His hand is now resting right on the number four!

Was it a coincidence that Mysto's hand ended up on the correct number? He calls for another helper and does it again. It works again. In fact, it even works when Mysto tries it with Mrs. Dexter, his teacher.

"Isn't it amazing," he explains, "how a clock can keep its hands over its face all the time and still be smarter than any of us? If you think it's me and not the clock that does this wonderful trick, let's see you do it, too."

How?

Surprisingly, this trick does work itself. It appears to be a real mystery, and your friends will not be able to figure it out; yet, it is an easy mathematical exercise. You will be able to understand it easily after you've done it a few times.

Here's the formula: After the number is secretly selected, you can begin your tapping anywhere you choose. Continue tapping any numbers you like for a total of *seven* taps. Then, and here is the real secret, tap number 12 on the eighth tap. Then tap backwards around the clock 11, 10, 9, 8, 7, 6 . . . and continue until the person says STOP. If he added one to his thought-of number with each of your taps, your hand will now be resting on his number when he says "20" in his mind. Why? Arithmetic! Try it right now with a clock drawn on a piece of scrap paper and see.

Do not repeat this too many times with the same audience. One or two times is fine. Three times should be the maximum. More than this and people will begin to realize that you eventually tap backwards from 12 and they may get wise to your method.

This trick can be as long or as short as you wish. If you repeat it several times it can get rather lengthy. If it does, it is important that your next trick be short and snappy so your audience resharpens its interest.

AN UPSIDE-DOWN SIX

Mysto shows a piece of cardboard with a big number 6 written on it.

"May I show you my favorite number . . . the number 6? There is one thing that has always fascinated me about it. It can be written like this (6) or like this."

He flips the card over to show the written word on the back, SIX. Then he turns the card back around so the 6 shows.

"Now there really is nothing very amazing about the number 6, or the written six except for this . . . if I turn the number 6 upside down, (he does) it becomes the number 9."

"And," he continues, "this is the most amazing thing of all; when the number 6 becomes a 9 by being turned upside down, the written SIX becomes a NINE also."

Mysto flips the card over and, rather than the word SIX on the back, the audience now sees the word NINE!

How?

Remember that this is a "quicky" trick. Do it fast and with few words. It serves to keep your audience on their toes and should make them wonder if what they think they saw really happened.

The trick is in the card. You will have to make it carefully, but it will last you for a long time and you will enjoy using it.

Obtain a piece of black cardboard about six inches long and eight inches high. You can make this by painting a sheet of white cardboard with black poster paint.

You will also require three sheets of heavy white paper. Each one will have to be about five by seven inches. All should be identical.

Glue a sheet of the white paper in the center of both the front and the back of the black cardboard, leaving about a half inch of black around the edge as a border. (See illustration on page 154.)

Fold the extra sheet of white paper in half several times. Apply glue to one side of this folded sheet. Glue it to one half of one of the white sheets on the black card. This will make a flap of white paper on one side. See the illustration on how this flap is made.

Using a dark colored felt-tipped pen, draw a big number 9 on the white side without the flap. Next turn the number 9 upside down, then turn the card over and, with the flap open, write SIX.

Keeping the side with the written SIX toward you, turn it upside down and close the flap. On the exposed side of the closed flap, write NINE. You are now ready to practice the trick in front of a mirror.

Pick up the card and hold it so the number is a 6 to the audience. The flap should be in position in the back so you can see the word SIX. Hold the flap in place with your thumb and fingers.

After showing the number 6, twist the card around to show the back, and the word SIX. Then turn the card front again to show the number 6.

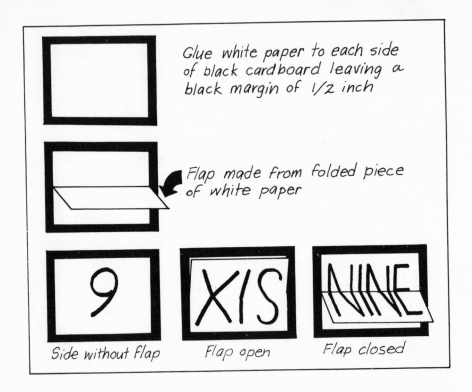

Glue white paper to each side of black cardboard leaving a black margin of 1/2 inch

Flap made from folded piece of white paper

Side without flap   Flap open   Flap closed

Next, twist the card around to turn the 6 upside down, thus changing it into the number 9. After you do this, with both hands, use your thumbs behind the card to flop the secret flap over so the word SIX is changed to NINE. This is done behind the card and will go unnoticed by your audience. But always watch your side angles!

Finally, turn the card around to show that the word NINE has mysteriously appeared on the back when you changed the 6 into the 9.

Do it quickly! Pretend that it is "only natural" and set the card aside. You may be sure that your audience will continue to puzzle over this mini-mystery long after you have performed it. After all, everyone knows that an upside-down 6 is a nine. Isn't it possible that it could work with words, too?

Although it is not a good idea to do two similar tricks in a row, such as two vanishes or two changes, it is sometimes nice in a theme show to continue with the same "reason" for a trick. For example, in his school show, Mysto might put several arithmetic ideas together. They would all work with numbers, yet are very different in effect. "An Upside-Down Six" is a comedy trick that is followed nicely by a number trick that looks far more difficult.

INSTANT ADDITION

Moving back to the blackboard, Mysto invites four helpers up to assist him.

"I would like to show you," he announces, "the famous 'Instant Addition' experiment . . . an exercise that will bring joy to Mrs. Dexter's heart!"

Turning to the first student he hands him a piece of chalk and asks him to write any five digit number on the blackboard.

He writes 35682. Under it Mysto writes 64317.

Mysto turns to the next student and asks him to write another five digit number under those already written. He writes 79032. The blackboard now looks like this:

$$35682$$
$$64317$$
$$79032$$

Mysto takes the chalk and writes 20967 at the bottom of the column. He hands the chalk to the third helper and invites him to add still another five digit number underneath. He writes 74562.

Immediately following the third helper's writing, Mysto draws a line under the column of figures and puts a big plus sign beside them. The board looks like this:

$$35682$$
$$64317$$
$$+\ 79032$$
$$20967$$
$$\underline{74562}$$

Mysto then starts to hand the piece of chalk to his last helper but he suddenly remembers something. He takes a piece of paper and writes something on it quickly; then he hands the folded paper to his teacher, Mrs. Dexter, and says, "Would you please keep the paper until the columns have been added?"

He hands the chalk to the last student with instructions to add the columns. He invites the student to ask the class to help with the addition to see how quickly they can do it.

For several minutes the audience shouts out sums as the helper adds with them. Finally the columns are totaled at 274560.

Turning to Mrs. Dexter, Mysto asks, "Will you please open the paper I gave you before we began the addition, and read it aloud?"

Mrs. Dexter reads, "The number will add up to exactly 274560—signed, Mysto!"

How?

This is a very easy mathematical trick. It all works because of the magical number nine.

After the first person writes his five digit number, you write a row underneath. All you must do is write numbers which will make each of his digits total nine.

For example,

Helper writes	35682
You write	64317
Which totals	99999

Of course you do the addition in your head and simply write 64317 beneath his numbers.

The next person then adds his five digit number. You must simply add another line which will make each of his digits also total nine.

For example,

Helper writes	79032
You write	20967
Which totals	99999

Finally, the third helper writes still another line of five digits under this. In our example, the third helper wrote 74562. *You do not write anything under this last number.*

The blackboard now looks like this:

35682	(Number written by helper #1)
64317	(Your number, to total 9's)
+79032	(Number written by helper #2)
20967	(Your number to total 9's)
74562	(Number written by helper #3)

To figure the answer immediately: Subtract two from the number written by helper #3. Then place a two in front of your new five-digit number.

For example:

74562   (number written by helper #3)

−2   (subtract 2)

74560   (new total to be written after a number 2)

274560 is the answer to the addition!

No matter what digits are selected this same formula will always give you the correct answer to the addition of the columns. Because the total will always be different you can repeat it again if you choose, but don't do it too many times or someone may eventually catch on.

Be careful that your teacher doesn't decide you are indeed the mathematical wizard of the class and expect all your papers to be perfect! If your class doesn't understand why you can't do all your mathematics that easily, just explain there is a magic trick to it—a math-magic arithma-trick!

One of the most surprising and puzzling tricks is one that is done without any special equipment. If the magician is able to pick up common items and perform his miracles, he is doing "real" magic. The following trick uses a common classroom material, colored construction paper . . . and that's all!

WHAT COLOR DOES THAT FEEL LIKE?

Mysto has one of the class members bring him four differently colored sheets of construction paper. Red, green, blue, and yellow are brought.

Mysto asks that they be rolled into rough balls. He then turns his back to the audience, but continues talking.

"Will you place any one of the colored balls in my hands behind my back. I will not look at it, but will conduct this experiment by feel alone. Also, please hide the other three balls so I will not catch any glimpse of them."

Still without turning around, Mysto continues talking as he rolls the ball about in his hands.

"Do you know that colors have special feelings? Each one is different. Red, for example, has a very smooth feel. Green is a bit rough. Blue is silky with just a touch of unevenness, and yellow feels like a canary feather. Of course, only a very few people in this world have fingers sensitive enough to identify colors by feel . . . I know of only three, a woman in Siberia, a mathematics teacher in Melbourne, Australia, and, naturally, The Great Mysto!"

For the first time Mysto faces the audience . . . with a tongue-in-cheek smile and a wink. Then he begins to concentrate. He removes one hand from behind his back, shows it quite empty, and raises it to his forehead to think.

"This feels like yellow!" he exclaims.

He removes the ball from behind his back and holds it up. It is yellow.

He quickly offers to repeat the experiment, turning his back. Another colored ball is handed him and, as before, he identifies it properly. The experiment is continued for several more tries. Each one is a success.

"Rather than look for a magic secret here," suggests Mysto as he prepares to move on to his next effect, "I hope you will try this experiment yourself. Perhaps you will find that you, too, have this uncanny gift of being able to feel colors with your fingertips. Remember that we have five senses and five fingers. Perhaps one of our fingers, like one of our senses, has sight."

How?

It is extremely doubtful that anyone will truly believe you are able to feel colors. Instead, they will be sure you are performing a clever magic trick and are somehow sneaking a peek at the color with your eyes. You are! But you must do the trick so well that you never get caught.

You will need several colors of construction paper. When they are brought to you be sure they are all the same size and the same texture and weight of paper. This way nobody will suspect there is something different about each one.

You may use any and as many colors as you choose. Do not watch them being rolled into balls. Turn your back and give directions.

When the audience indicates that the balls are rolled, instruct them to put one into your hands behind your back. Take the ball with both hands . . . this is important.

After talking back to the audience for a few moments turn and face them. As soon as the ball is out of sight of the audience, simply tear off a very tiny piece of the paper and poke it under one of your fingernails.

As you talk, remove the hand with the hidden bit of paper and leave the ball in the hand behind your back. Casually open your hand to show it is empty (the audience will never see the tiny piece under your nail). Then place this hand to your forehead as though you were concentrating instead of doing what you are really doing—peeking at the bit of paper to see what color it is!

The trick is done. You can name the color of the ball behind your back. Drop the tiny bit on the floor and ask the audience to try again. You can repeat this several more times, but please do not overdo it. Finally suggest to your audience that they try it themselves or . . .

"Sorry, I just can't continue. My fingers are so tired I just have to rest them until I can put some eye drops on them."

If you know your audience very well, it is very important that you include a trick or routine where you all have fun together. This does not always have to be a magic trick, but if it fools your audience it will fit in nicely. The following works very well in a classroom.

A FOREIGN LANGUAGE CLASS

"One important subject in school," explains The Great Mysto, "is learning foreign languages. I would, therefore, like to give you a quick lesson in the strange language of the Molla Mollian tribe of the northern South Sea Islands. One of the most famous chants of the Molla Mollians is to their God of Dawn. It consists of only three words . . . easily learned. Every morning, upon rising, each Molla Mollian steps from his hut and shouts his chant skyward. It is this strange but haunting chant that I would like to teach you."

Mysto turns toward the blackboard. Picking up a stick of chalk, he writes:

OWA

"Please pronounce this with me. Say *Oh Wah,*" explains Mysto as he encourages the students to join him in saying the word. He has them repeat it several times, correcting them when they say it wrong, and complimenting them, finally, by telling them they sound like real **Molla Mollians.**

"Now try this word," says Mysto, turning to the blackboard. He writes: (Under OWA)

TAFOO

The students repeat the new word as Mysto explains that it should be pronounced in two syllables *Ta* and *Foo* . . . *Ta Foo.* It is quickly learned, and sounds so silly the audience finds it fun to say aloud in unison.

"Now for the final word in the sunrise chant to the God of Dawn," says Mysto as he turns and writes: (Under the two other words.)

LIAM

"This word is pronounced *Lie Am.* Please say it aloud."

The audience again practices the new word until Mysto, like a teacher, agrees that they have mastered it.

"Now imagine," he continues, "that one day you have the wonderful opportunity to actually visit one of these big tiny northern South Sea Islands, and you run across a tribe of Molla Mollians. Do you realize that you now know enough Molla Mollian words to shout out their sunrise chant which will let them know instantly what kind of person you are?"

"Just for practice, pretend that I am a handsome Molla Mollian and you are a visiting missionary. You are anxious to be my friend so you shout out your chant. Let me hear you do it—three times loudly."

The audience screams out, "OWA TAFOO LIAM, OWA TAFOO LIAM, OWA TAFOO LIAM." They may think it is foolish, but it's great fun!

"And," continues Mysto, "if I were that Molla Mollian I'd probably answer you in this way . . . *you certainly are. In fact, I never knew before how many fools there are in my classroom.*"

How?

With just a silly story and a few misspelled words you have your entire class shouting "Oh what a fool I am," without even knowing they are doing it.

Just be sure you write the three words in big bold letters on the blackboard in the correct way:

OWA

TAFOO

LIAM

Be sure that your last statement about "never knew there were so many fools in my classroom" is heard by everybody. Your sentence, at first, will not make any sense but slowly they will "catch on."

One by one the students will understand and read the words properly; then they will explain it to the "slow learners" and pretty soon everyone will be laughing. You will have pulled off a real class-sized joke but, unfortunately, you will never be able to use it on your class again. Maybe you won't even be able to use it in your town again because everyone will be trying it on their parents and friends. Your joke will be spoiled . . . but there will be many more audiences for you to "make fools of."

Now for a finale . . . the end trick. It does not have to be a "big number" because you will not be able to bow and have the curtains close to leave the audience with only memories. After your final trick you will simply be back in class surrounded by your friends. Your last trick should just leave the audience with a laugh . . . and a little mystery. Mysto likes the next mystery because it involves homework and homework is usually the teacher's last "trick" also.

MYSTO DOES HIS HOMEWORK

Picking up a notebook Mysto asks, "Do you know what is best about being a magician? It is being able to fool people. In fact, sometimes you can even fool a teacher!"

The audience chuckles. They like that idea, being able to fool a teacher. Mysto continues.

"Let me tell you a story about how magic really did help me fool a teacher once. She had given us an assignment. We were to write a story about whomever we considered to be the most famous person in the world. I brought my notebook home to do it, but I just couldn't decide on the person. George Washington, Abraham Lincoln, Queen Elizabeth, Cleopatra, Helen Keller, Albert Einstein . . . there were so many to choose from. Finally I forgot about the whole thing and went to bed. When I got to school the next day my notebook was blank, just like this one."

Mysto flips through the pages of the notebook he has been holding and shows them to the audience. Every page is perfectly blank.

"Now I was really worried. In just a few minutes Mrs. Eaglebeak, my teacher, would call for the homework and my notebook . . . like my mind . . . was a perfect blank! Then suddenly it hit me. I knew just what to do. Quickly I pulled out my trusty pencil and used it . . . not for writing, but for a magic wand. I waved it frantically back and forth over the empty notebook and chanted my magic spell: Hocus Pocus, pudding and pie, do my homework or I will die."

As Mysto talks he is doing the things he describes in his story. He has waved the pencil over the notebook he has shown empty. Now he continues to tell the story and act it out.

"Do you know what happened? My magic came through again and completed my homework assignment in less time than it took Mrs. Eaglebeak to sharpen her pencil so she could give me an 'A' for it!"

Mysto flips through the pages very slowly. Every page is now filled with writing on both sides.

"And, naturally, now you know exactly whom I wrote

my assignment about . . . the most famous person in the world . . . er, excuse me, the most famous *magician* in the world!"

He continues flipping through the pages, showing them all filled with writing, until he reaches the title page. There, in big bold, letters is:

MYSTO THE MAGICIAN
BY
MYSTO THE MAGICIAN

How?

The secret is in the notebook. Shop around in the stationery department of any variety store until you find one that works well. Look for an inexpensive notebook with spiral bindings and pages that can be torn out easily. The pages should open out flat when the book is laid flat on a tabletop. The book should have pages at least eight by ten inches, so everyone can see them easily.

When you find a good notebook it must be carefully prepared. Once it is done, however, it will last for many, many shows.

First, tear out all except 15 sheets (30 pages). Next, with a ruler make a light pencil line down the edge of every page one-half inch in. Cut off this half inch strip on *every other* page. First page one, then on page three, then page five, etc. Continue to cut the strip off every other page throughout the whole book.

Now, open the notebook to the first side of page one and write THE GREAT MYSTO by THE GREAT MYSTO in bold letters with a felt-tipped marking pen. (Naturally, if your name is not Mysto you should use your own.)

To do the following properly, you might like to number all the pages in the notebook, lightly with pencil, in a corner. The first page is the "title" page, so flip it over and put "1" on the back of the first page. The front side of the next sheet will be "2" and the back side "3" and so on through the book.

Follow the chart below to see which pages to scribble on (or "write" your make-believe homework assignment) and which pages to leave blank.

Write on these pages		Leave these pages blank	
1	17	3	19
2	18	4	20
5	21	7	23
6	22	8	24
9	25	11	27
10	26	12	28
13	29	15	
14		16	

If this sounds a little confusing, let me assure you it will make very good sense if you obtain a notebook and actually follow the directions in preparing it. All you are really doing is writing on every other two pages and every other page is cut a bit shorter.

One last thing: Both covers of the notebook, front and back, must look exactly the same. You must be able to show either and call it the "cover."

When you have completed gimmicking the notebook you are ready to experiment a bit and really learn how easily the trick works.

Set it down on the table with the title page (MYSTO THE MAGICIAN BY MYSTO THE MAGICIAN) down toward the table. Make a pencil dot on the book cover so you can always put it down this way.

Pick up the notebook and lay it flat in your left hand. Grasp the edge with your right hand and flip it open using your right thumb. You will automatically open to an empty page!

It will be empty if your right thumb opens the book because every short page will fall down and your thumb will "catch" one of the long pages. Try it . . . you'll see it happens almost by itself!

If you do it this way your audience will be thoroughly convinced that you are holding only an empty notebook.

Finally, to make the writing appear just close the book and, casually, turn it upside down. Flip through the pages again (now the "back" cover has become the "front") in the same way. This time the long pages will stop the short pages and, by magic it appears, the pages will all be filled with writing.

To end the trick, simply keep flipping until you reach the title page showing the MYSTO THE MAGICIAN BY MYSTO THE MAGICIAN.

Your time is well spent in making this notebook. It requires a lot of work on your part, but, amazingly, you will create a trick which will work itself.

But be careful. Like all self-working tricks you must understand it well. One wrong move and you can spoil it. Do not be charmed by its simplicity. Learn one thing well: how to flip the pages. If you spend a few hours learning it, and several shows doing it, you will find you can do this trick almost without thinking from then on.

There really is nothing special about the above trick that makes it work particularly well in school except for the story. Mysto would be the first to remind you that any of the tricks in this chapter could be done at any show, anywhere. A really clever magician can adapt tricks and stories to fit any situation. Suppose, for example, you were asked to do a few tricks for a boy or girl scout group. Could you make some of your tricks into a "theme" show for that particular group? Try to make up such an imaginary show right now. The time may come soon for you to really do it.

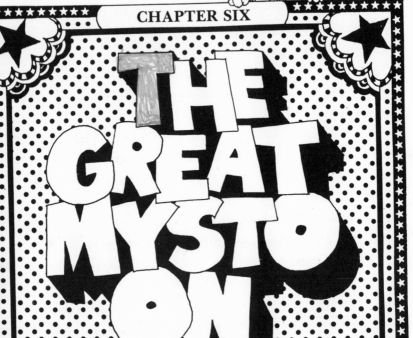

CHAPTER SIX

THE GREAT MYSTO ON STAGE

Every magician dreams of presenting an act on a real stage, with real curtains, lights, and an assistant or two. Unfortunately, most magic shows are given at parties or for small groups of people gathered in a room. Small rooms and small groups are a magician's training ground. Here he learns his craft and becomes an expert entertainer.

The time will come when people know The Great Mysto well enough to invite him to entertain a group from a stage. Perhaps it will be a church group, a school assembly, a club meeting, or it might be a "Talent Show" you would like to enter. Whatever it is that allows you to go on a real stage and do a magic show for a large gathering of people is a golden opportunity. Will you be ready for it?

This chapter will present a stage-size magic show, just as it could be done by The Great Mysto. You will find that the tricks follow one another in a logical way and that they include a good deal of variety. You can include other tricks, if you wish, when you present your stage show. Remember though, the tricks must be large enough so everyone can see from the very back of the hall and they must be *very entertaining* so every person in your audience will be interested.

One word of caution! If it is to be on a real stage check the whole situation beforehand. See if all the audience will be in front of you and not on the sides, if there is a curtain that closes, and if there is a space to set up in privacy.

One advantage you will have on stage is being able to hide things easily in the "wings" of the stage. Your assistant can bring them in as you require them. Angles are no problem. With everyone sitting in front, nobody can see from the sides or back. Finally, when the show is done, the curtains can close as you take your bow.

But first things first. Before they close, the curtains must open and things must happen: Mysto's magic tricks and showmanship.

THE GREAT MYSTO AND COMPANY

The show is about to begin. The audience is waiting for The Great Mysto to appear. The curtains open just a bit . . . but it is not The Great Mysto; it is his assistant.

The assistant comes out on the apron of the stage (the part in front of the curtains) and is seen holding a small wooden tripod and some big sheets of cardboard. The audience watches with interest. The assistant goes to one side of the apron and sets the tripod in place. Then he places the cards on the stand and turns one around. It reads:

> **THE GREAT MYSTO**
> **AND**
> **COMPANY**

Without saying a word, the assistant points to the word **COMPANY**, then points to himself . . . smiles and bows. Then he starts to walk away when . . . CRASH . . . the whole stand and the cards spill over in a mess.

Slowly, with great embarrassment, he walks back and sets the cards back on the stand. Then he slowly . . . sadly . . . turns another card around. It reads:

> **THE GREAT MYSTO**
> **and**
> **company**

With that he walks off the stage amidst the audience's laughter.

How?

No magic, just an unexpected introduction to the show. You will need a simple wooden tripod, or any kind of stand that will hold a number of cards.

The cards should be as large as possible. In all, you will require four signs plus one blank card. The four signs should be lettered in dark paint as follows:

THE GREAT MYSTO AND THE GREAT COMPANY	THE GREAT MYSTO AND COMPANY
mysto and company	THE GREAT MYSTO and company

The signs should be stacked up with the blank card in front. Sign #1 is behind the blank card, and sign #4 is last. For this introduction you will use only the first two signs; the others will be used later in the show.

Follow the description above to learn the routine. The only magic is making the tripod fall over when the assistant walks away. This is easily accomplished by tying a short length of thread from the tripod to the assistant's ankle. He carries the tripod in and sets it up. Then, as he walks away, the thread tugs it over automatically. The thread is easily broken as the assistant sets things back in place.

This "opening" is actually the beginning of a short "running gag" that is going to continue until the very end of the show. Once you learn how the gag works you might want to make up other signs and insert them in other places as well.

MYSTO'S FISHY ENTRANCE

The curtains open. The audience sees Mysto's assistant standing smartly at attention. His right hand is held in front, with a cloth draped over it. His left hand is held behind his back. Suddenly he extends the arm with the cloth draped over it and points to the stage wing. Mysto enters.

Walking quickly to the assistant, he removes the cloth and flings it to and fro to display both sides. He returns one corner to the assistant's hand, and he holds the other. They hold the cloth opened in a square between them. Mysto holds up his free hand and waves it back and forth.

Suddenly he reaches quickly behind the cloth and moves his hand forward. A shape is seen under the material. Immediately, Mysto walks forward as the assistant releases his corner. In the center of the stage . . . right under the very noses of his audience . . . Mysto pulls the cloth away. He is holding a large clear goldfish bowl! It is filled with real water and has real goldfish swimming about inside.

The assistant has left the stage, but now returns with a small table containing some objects. He sets the table down as Mysto hands him the bowl.

Before his assistant leaves with the bowl, Mysto picks a drinking glass off the table and scoops out a glassful of water from the bowl. He pours a bit out to show the audience that it is real water; then he sets the glass on the table to be used in his next trick.

How?

To do this trick you must have a large cloth, a goldfish bowl (preferably plastic), a few goldfish, a stage, some nerve, and . . . most important of all . . . an assistant that you can depend on thoroughly. It is your trusty assistant, not you, who really does this trick! Naturally, you must help too, and you both must practice together as a team many times.

Get a small goldfish bowl. By trying the trick a few times you can decide just how big it should be. The scarf can be a 36 inch square bandana from a variety store. The cloth must be heavy enough so the audience can't see through it.

You can use goldfish if you wish, but the trick will work just as well without them. You don't even need the water. One magician happened to have some baby kittens so he put one of those in the bowl. It was very, very effective. The main reason Mysto uses water is that he is going to require some for his next trick.

Your assistant must be in his place, holding the scarf and the bowl, before the curtains open. He holds the bowl in his left hand behind his back, and the scarf tossed over his right hand in front. The illustration on page 182 will show you how he should appear.

Mysto, if there is no "stage crew," must open the curtains.

As the curtains open, have your assistant stand stiffly at attention. This way, the position of his hands will look formal, but natural.

As you walk on, he extends his right arm *to the left* and points to you. (You must enter on his left side.) Take the scarf off his arm and show both sides of it quickly.

Place one corner back in his right hand and you hold the opposite corner so it hangs down in a large square between you both. You should be standing to the assistant's left and holding the cloth with your left hand.

Show that your right hand is empty and quickly reach under the cloth from the rear. At the same moment your assistant moves the bowl into position behind the cloth where you can get it. His left hand and movements are hidden behind the cloth.

As soon as you have the bowl, your assistant must return his left hand to the same position behind his back. He then releases the cloth as you walk forward to make your production.

As you walk forward, the assistant can drop both arms by his side and walk off stage to get set up for the next trick.

Practice this trick well. As a team, you and your assistant can produce almost anything the occasion demands: a live rabbit, a birthday cake, a trophy for a banquet, or a bouquet of flowers for a special person.

Mysto then goes quickly from this trick into his next. Having dipped out a glassful of water, he has already begun. Also, for his next trick, he speaks. Some magicians do their act in complete silence and use body movement and facial expressions. This is called *pantomime*. But most young magicians do much better when they use words.

THE SURPRISE SNOWSTORM

Holding a sheet of colored tissue paper, Mysto tears it into tiny shreds. He does the same with another sheet of a different color. And still another.

"I'm going to show you how a magician is able to create an instant snowstorm. First, you need a little water."

Mysto dips the torn bits of tissue into the glass of water resting on his table. He soaks the paper thoroughly and squeezes it so the audience can see the water drip off.

He places the wet mass of paper in his left hand and picks up a Chinese fan in his right hand.

"Next, we require a bit of cool air."

Opening the fan, Mysto begins to wave it back and forth toward his left hand.

"And . . . you get a surprise snowstorm."

Slowly he opens his left hand and bits of dry paper begin to fly away. He continues fanning and opening his hand as a great cloud of dry confetti snow whirls from his hand.

Finally he opens his hand to show it is empty. It appears that Mysto was able to produce dry paper snow from what had only one moment before been a wet, soggy mess of torn tissues.

How?

This is a beautiful trick, and you will find it beautifully simple to perform. It will require that you practice doing the right things at the right time.

You will need a glass of water, a small Chinese fan (buy one or fold one from a sheet of heavy colored paper), several sheets of colored tissue paper, and some dry confetti.

The confetti is hidden in a special bundle. Cut a square of colored tissue 2½ inches square and lay it flat on the table. Pour a heap of confetti in the middle. Bring up the corners and twist them together to make a tiny bundle of colored confetti. To make it easier to break open at the proper time, cut several short gashes in it with scissors. This bundle is placed on your table with some object in front to hide it from view.

On the table, too, are the glass of water, the fan, and several sheets of differently colored tissues. To perform the trick, first pick up the tissue sheets one at a time. Show them and tear them into pieces. Don't bother to tear them too small; in fact leaving them big will enhance the mystery when the tiny confetti "snow" appears.

Gather all the torn pieces and wad them into a ball. Hold the ball in your *right hand* and show it; then dip it into the water. Dip it several times, making sure everyone sees what you are doing and realizes that the papers really are getting very wet.

While you are dipping the tissue, place your left hand on the table *right over the hidden confetti bundle* and catch it in your left palm, holding it in place with your thumb. Keep the back of your left hand toward the audience so nobody sees the bundle.

Hold the soaked ball up in your right hand. Show it and squeeze a little water out of it. Be sure everyone sees.

Now, and here is a part you must practice, pretend to place the wet ball into your left hand but really keep it in your right. This is easy to do and you do not really have to do it very well because nobody will really watch very carefully. After all, all you are doing is "changing hands," and that doesn't seem very important. Keep your left hand, with the dry bundle, closed in a fist and open your right hand a bit as though it were empty. (Just hold the wet bundle against your palm with your thumb and keep the back of your hand toward the audience.)

As soon as you have done this, raise your left hand, with the dry bundle, high in the air, and with your right hand reach for the fan on the table. As you pick up the fan, drop the wet ball on the table. If your audience can see the top of the table, have the fan in a small box so when reaching in for it, you leave the ball inside.

Now the trick is done, but, like all good tricks, the audience still doesn't know what is going to happen. Probably many people will expect you to restore the tissues to whole sheets again. Nobody will expect what is about to happen.

Fan your left hand and, as you do, break the bundle open with your thumb. Allow some confetti to blow away. Continue to fan and open your hand. Go slowly and you can keep the "snowstorm" going for a surprisingly long period of time and there will appear to be much more snow than there actually is.

At the end, show your empty hands. You can do this because even the tissue paper wrapping on the bundle will blow away in the "storm" and nobody will even notice it!

A magician, particularly on a stage, should be a magician every minute. Things which are quite impossible should be done as-a-matter-of-fact. The following is a trick that is not a trick. It is just something Mysto would do if he were indeed a real magician.

BOY IS IT HOT IN HERE

Naturally, for his stage appearance, Mysto is wearing a jacket and a necktie.

"Boy, after that snowstorm, is it ever hot in here!" he says as he takes his Chinese fan and fans his own face. He looks very uncomfortable.

"If any of you folks are uncomfortable please feel free to take off your sweaters, jackets, or shoes . . . er, well, perhaps you had best leave your shoes on and leave the smelling to your noses!"

Mysto continues to fan and look very hot.

"Would anyone mind if I removed my necktie?" he asks. "It will only take a moment."

Mysto reaches up, grabs his necktie by the middle, and gives it a sudden pull. The tie comes *right through his neck* with the loop still tied. Mysto looks at it for a moment so everyone sees.

"Ah . . . much better!"

How?

If you don't own a necktie, buy one, and save it. It will be a magic prop you can use in this trick and you will really enjoy doing it. The trick is extremely simple and very startling. It also lets you begin your show well-dressed and still allows you to finish in "bare-necked" comfort!

It is a quick trick done not as a trick at all, but as simply the way any magician would make himself more comfortable. Please do not expect, or make, people applaud, because it is not meant to be a "big" trick. Magicians call this

kind of gag a "throw-away." It takes only a moment but makes some people wonder for a long, long time.

How do you do it? Tie a tie about your neck using any standard knot. Have your dad or a friend do it if you don't know how. Next loosen the tie so you can slip it off over your head. The tie is still tied; once it is off your head, tighten the loop so it is about as big around as your neck. This is your prop tie. Keep it just like this for use whenever you want it.

To use: flatten the loop and tuck it under your collar on both sides. The illustrations will show you how. From the front it looks like any other tie, but it goes only halfway around your neck.

You wear it like this until you're ready. Then you reach up, grab the tie, and give a quick pull. The tie slips out from under your collar and the loop will open out as though it penetrated right through your neck. Try it once in front of a mirror and you will appreciate how unbelievable it appears!

A magic show can be done in either of two ways: It can be a series of different, unrelated magic tricks done one after another, or it can be a "routine." This is where each trick seems to be part of every other trick and one thing blends logically into something else. Routines are much more magical, because it gives an audience the feeling that you are doing magic with anything you touch. For example, rather than just lay your necktie aside after pulling it off, you might logically do a trick with it.

THE NECKTIE SNAKE

After removing his necktie and untying it, Mysto looks at it for a moment.

"Did you ever have trouble tying a necktie?" he asks. "I always have trouble tying mine, but I have learned a great secret! It is much easier to *untie* one! In fact, a magician can make a necktie untie itself."

Mysto ties a loose knot in the middle of his necktie which he holds by the big end, letting the small end hang down. The knot is in the middle.

"All I have to do is hypnotize my necktie and make it think that it is a snake. As you all know, snakes don't like to be tied in knots."

Mysto makes a few mystical passes toward the tie with his free hand, and says, "You are not a necktie; you are a snake. You are not a necktie in a knot; you are a snake in a knot that does not want to be naughty."

Suddenly the lower end of the necktie begins to move and curl upward.

"Watch!" orders Mysto.

The bottom creeps up into the knot, passes through it, and creeps back down . . . untying the knot!

Laying the tie aside, Mysto warns the audience; "If you try this trick, just be sure you remove the hypnotic spell from the necktie before you use it again. Imagine putting a snake around your neck and tying it in a knot . . . I can assure you that snakes don't like that one little bit!"

How?

First, get a silk or nylon tie, one that is made of very smooth cloth. The tie must be prepared before you come on stage. The gimmick is a length of black thread and a dark-colored button.

With a needle, attach one end of the thread to the very tip of the narrow end of the necktie. Be sure to attach it securely by sewing it through several times and then tying it in place.

Next you must tie the button on the other end of the thread. How long should the thread be? It depends on how tall you are. You will have to determine this by experimenting.

Hold the small end of the tie in your hand with the big end hanging down. The thread will hang down alongside the necktie. Now tie a big *loose* knot in the middle of the tie (with the thread going inside the knot too . . . just tie both the tie and the thread at the same time). Then hold the *big* end of the tie out at arm's length and let the small end, and the thread end, hang down. Now cut the thread where it touches the floor and tie on the button.

Not only are you now able to tie the button on the right length thread, but you are also ready to see the trick work. Simply step on the button with your foot and lift the tie up slowly while holding on to the big end. The thread will tug on the bottom end of the tie, and it will be pulled up. The

String   Button

end of the tie along with the thread will pass through the knot as you continue to pull the tie upward. Finally, as the end passes through the knot, it will curl back down toward the floor in the direction of the thread.

The first time you try it, it may not work as easily as it sounds. You must not tie the knot too tightly or the end will not be able to worm its way through. Try it several times and you will finally learn to control your necktie snake so that it looks very much alive. You'll find it is really fun to practice even though you know very well how it is done.

When you first come onstage wearing the necktie, the thread and button are simply hanging down, or the button can be in your pocket with the thread hanging out. After you remove the tie, it is a very simple matter to move the thread and button into position for the trick. When the button is on the floor, just step on it, take the tie by the small end, and tie your knot with the thread inside.

One final note: Some young magicians are very frightened to use any trick that involves a thread. They are sure the audience will see it. This is not true, particularly on a stage. Have your assistant try it while you sit nearby and you will discover a thread is almost invisible. Also, remember that the thread comes from underneath, but the tie moves up . . . the audience will be looking for something in the tie or your hand . . . certainly not for a thread from your foot! There is an old saying about magic: "It's all done with mirrors and black thread." Actually, so few tricks are done with these things, that it's kind of fun to do one once in a while.

Do you like to experiment? Many magicians don't use black thread. They even argue about what color shows up the least from a stage. Many prefer dark brown thread. Black thread was used when magicians wore black dress tuxedoes. Why don't you experiment on your own! There are all colors available, even threads made of nylon with no color at all. Visit the thread counter of your local sewing supply center and shop around; just tell the salesman that you are a magician and you're looking over their supply of "black thread"—see if he believes you!

Tricks which use members of the audience are well liked. It is important to use at least one in every show you do. The following is a fine example of a very old "classic" trick which has astounded spectators for years. Usually, card tricks done from a stage are not recommended . . . but this one is a knockout!

THE THREE CARDS ACROSS

"I will require two people onstage to help me," says Mysto as he picks up a pack of playing cards. "These two people must be expert mathematicians. By that, I mean they must be capable of counting up to at least ten."

Two people are selected. They stand one on each side of Mysto. He hands one the deck of cards and says, "Would you please count the cards?"

The helper counts them aloud and finds exactly 20.

"Please hand ten to your helper here," Mysto says. "Now, take your remaining ten cards and bring them right down into the audience. Allow three people to select one card apiece and remember it. Then shuffle the selected cards back into the deck and return here."

While the helper is down having the cards selected, Mysto works with the spectator still onstage. He is holding the pack of cards.

"Would you please count your cards down on the table to be sure you have exactly ten."

The helper counts. As he does, Mysto picks up a stack of envelopes. When the spectator has counted his last card, Mysto tosses an envelope on top and asks him to seal his cards in it. When this has been done he is asked to hold the envelope tightly and in plain view of the audience at all times. He then asks this assistant to stand to one side of the stage.

The helper in the audience is now finished and returns to the stage. As he returns, Mysto takes his packet of cards and seals them in an envelope. The sealed envelope is handed to this helper to hold on the other side of the stage.

"Now," explains Mysto, "I will do the impossible! I will make the three selected cards fly, invisibly, from the packet they were selected from to the packet that was sealed in the envelope while they were being selected."

Mysto asks the first spectator who chose a card to name it. He then asks the card to "fly" from envelope to envelope. He repeats this with the other two selected cards. Turning to the helper who had the cards selected, Mysto says, "Now, if you had ten cards, but I made three fly away, how many are left in your envelope now?"

"Seven," suggests the helper with a grin.

"Correct!" roars Mysto. "Open your envelope and count your cards."

While this is started, Mysto turns immediately to the other helper, and says, "And you must have three extra cards in your envelope if I made them fly there. How many will that make?"

"Thirteen," says the helper, not believing it is possible.

"Then you open the envelope and count, too," orders Mysto.

By this time the first helper has finished counting and has found only seven cards. Mysto asks him to name the cards aloud and he asks the spectators who selected the three cards to listen for their cards. They never hear them—the selected cards are gone!

"Remember," exclaims The Great Mysto, "we had only 20 cards and I have not been near either of the packets of ten. My helpers did all the work for me and you watched very carefully. Yet, I have made three cards change places . . . and you selected which three were to go. Let's see if they did."

Mysto turns to the second helper. He has counted his cards . . . and found 13! Mysto asks for the names of the selected cards again while the helper looks through the packet. All three selected cards are there!

"Thank you," says Mysto to his helpers as he sends them back to their seats. "And, if anyone thinks there is anything special about the cards or the envelopes . . . I'll just give them to my helpers to keep and you can see them after the show and examine the cards and envelopes (not the helpers) to your heart's content!"

How?

Does this trick sound impossible to you? If so, you can be sure it will look impossible to your audience, also. Because it is such a fine trick, it is well worth the time, preparation, and nerve you will need to present it! It is not a simple "self-working" trick and many beginning magicians will probably say it is too hard and look for some simpler effect. This is exactly why a *real* magician, like Mysto, will learn it well. It is just intricate enough to completely fool anyone in your audience who has skimmed through a magic book or two and thinks he knows how all the tricks work.

You will need several things that require a bit of special gimmicking:

1. Purchase two identical decks of playing cards. Make a stack of ten cards from each deck. The two stacks should contain duplicate cards. Place one stack on top of the other.

2. A stack of six ordinary white envelopes. One is prepared by simply cutting off the triangular flap that is sealed down.

3. Place seven odd cards in the top envelope (be sure they are not duplicates of any in the stack of 20 cards).

4. In front of the envelope on top (containing the seven odd cards) place the flapless envelope. See illustration on page 200.

5. Place a rubber band around the pack of envelopes. Place three odd cards (not duplicates of any in the card stack) on the bottom of the pack of envelopes under the rubber band.

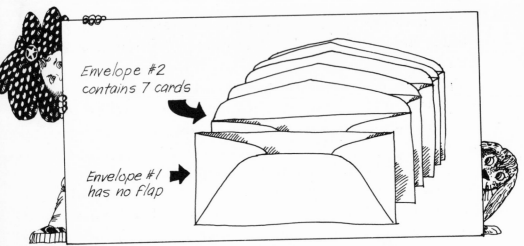

Envelope #2 contains 7 cards

Envelope #1 has no flap

You are now ready to do the trick. But first you must practice it until you can do it very smoothly. Invite up two helpers and hand one the stack of 20 cards. Ask him to count them aloud and to place them on the table. Then he is to pick them up and count off ten for the other helper. It is important that all the counting be done *facedown* so nobody knows the names of any cards yet.

Send the first helper into the audience with his pack of ten cards and ask him to have three selected. It makes no difference which three are chosen so let him do it on his own, but be sure he has them chosen from the *facedown* pack so only the three cards selected are ever seen.

Turn to the other helper while the cards are being selected and ask him to count his cards—*facedown,* one at a time on the table.

While he does this, pick up the stack of envelopes and slip off the rubber band. Remove the bottom envelope in the stack, while keeping the three cards hidden underneath.

As soon as he has completed his counting, casually drop the envelope *right on top of the pile on the table.* This adds three cards to the ten he has placed there. This requires nerve, but it is very simple and your helper will never notice the extra cards. Be sure to tell him to, "Hurry and seal them in this envelope," as you lay it down.

Send this helper with his packet of 13 cards, that he thinks contains ten, over to one side of the stage. The other helper should be coming back from the audience with his stack of ten cards. If not, hurry him up.

As he returns, hold up the stack of envelopes with the flap side facing you. Take his stack of cards as he approaches and slip them into the "top" envelope of the stack. Actually they slip into the flapless envelope.

Next take hold of the first flap and pull the envelope out. If you are following this carefully, you know that you have really pulled out the *second* envelope containing the seven odd cards, and left the flapless envelope with the ten cards on top of the envelope stack.

Immediately hand this envelope, with the cards, to the helper and ask that he "seal the cards inside and hold on to the envelope."

Properly done, this switch of cards will never be seen or even suspected. Later, people will swear that you never even got near the cards, but that your helpers did everything.

You are now ready for the trick to begin . . . as far as the audience sees it. Actually, the trick is all done as far as your "trickery" is concerned. Be sure you do not get near either helper from now on. Let them do all the work.

Ask the names of the three selected cards. Wave your hand mysteriously and ask the cards to fly invisibly from envelope to envelope. Finally ask that the envelopes be opened and the cards be checked. The seven cards in one will not contain those that were chosen, but the 13 in the other will. To an audience this will be real magic. Nobody will be able to explain it but everybody will be sure to talk about it. And be sure to keep it a real secret; this is not a trick that anyone can do.

Comedy should play an important part in any stage magic show presented by a young magician. An occasional "real" mystery like THE THREE CARDS ACROSS proves you are a fine magician but always remember that an audience likes to laugh. Follow a mystery with a bit of humor.

FLOWERS FROM INDIA

Mysto tells an unusual story.

"I have always been interested in magic from India . . . the rope trick, snake charmers, and fakirs who remain buried alive for days. For my next trick I would like to show you a mystery I picked up on my last trip there . . . when nobody was looking! I call this trick the GROWTH OF THE SACRED FLOWERS. It goes like this . . ."

Mysto takes out a flower pot, shows it is empty, and proceeds to fill it with dirt from a paper bag.

"The Hindu mystic begins with a simple clay pot which he fills with dirt . . . sacred dirt dug from under the fingernails of the High Lama."

He reaches into his pocket and removes a small envelope. He reaches inside and takes out a large seed which he plants in the flowerpot.

"Now we plant a seed from the magical Lotus Tree in the sacred dirt. The Lotus needs only three things to grow into a beautiful flower . . ."

Mysto sprinkles a bit of water from a fancy vase into the pot, and continues, "First a bit of holy water from the Ganges River during a full moon. Now, a bit of air."

Mysto picks up the pot and raises and lowers it several times, holding it with both hands. He then places it back on the table.

"And thirdly, unlike most plants, the Sacred Lotus Tree must have the peace of darkness. The Lotus is the only flower known that will bloom in total darkness. The Hindus say it blooms and grows only in the dark because it is looking for the light, which is easy to understand. Let me show you . . ."

He picks up a square cloth and holds it with a corner in each hand. It is flipped back and forth several times to show both sides. Mysto then holds it in front of the flowerpot for a moment so it covers the pot like a curtain.

"In this short period of darkness the Sacred Lotus seed has sprouted, grown stems and leaves, and finally flowered to produce a breathtaking plant that is more beautiful than any other in the world. . . . BEHOLD!"

Mysto flips the cloth aside. Standing in the pot is a plant—the leaves are withered and ragged, the stem is broken and twisted, and there are no flowers at all. It is very sad . . . the audience laughs.

"I'm sorry," explains Mysto. "Perhaps I should have spent more time with the Hindu mystic who taught me that trick. I should not have tried to learn it in his correspondence course. Ah, well . . ."

Mysto walks slowly over to the sign his assistant set up at the start of the show. It now reads:

> **THE GREAT MYSTO**
> **and**
> **company**

Mysto removes that sign and sets it behind the cards. The new sign reads:

> **mysto**
> **and**
> **company**

The Great Mysto has admitted that he is no longer **"GREAT"** . . . the audience laughs (which is what you really want, isn't it?).

How?

Do this trick quite quickly. Overact when you tell your story. Be very dramatic. Make it sound as though you are going to do great things. This in itself, will make the audience laugh and it will make your "failure" even funnier.

You will need: a clay flowerpot, a bag with some soil (gravel or pebbles work well too and are not as messy), an envelope containing a "Lotus Seed" (any big seed or smooth rock), a specially prepared cloth, and a Lotus Tree.

Make the Lotus Tree out of a real bush. Choose a twig (perhaps a foot high) with big leaves. Break a few branches, but don't remove them. Use scissors to cut holes and pieces out of the leaves. Do anything you can to make it look awful! (If you prefer you can buy a plastic "flower" and do the same thing to it. The plastic one will last for many shows.)

The cloth must be prepared. Use a heavy scarf about three feet square. It must be thick enough so your audience can't see through it. To "gimmick" it, push a straight pin through one corner and bend the point over with a pair of pliers. Sew a few stitches around it to hold it in place. The illustration will show you how this is done. In doing the trick, the cloth is folded so the hook is on top and you can grab it easily with your hand.

Have all the objects used in the trick on your table, except for the Lotus Tree. This is hidden under your coat on the left side. To keep the bush in place, so it doesn't fall out the bottom of your jacket, pin a safety pin to the inside of your jacket up under the armpit. Attach the top of the bush to the pin with a rubber band. When you put on the coat, the bush will hang down from the pin and be pressed flat against your body. Nobody will see it or know that it's there, but when you want it you can pull it free from the rubber band easily and quickly.

(Note: The following directions are for a righthanded magician, *if you are left-handed,* simply exchange "right" for "left" in the directions. Begin with the tree under your *right* side.)

Follow the above description of the trick: Show the pot and fill it with soil; plant the seed and wave the pot in the air; finally pick up the cloth.

Pick the cloth up, holding the hook in your right hand and the opposite corner in your left. Flip it back and forth to display each side.

Finally, cross your arms with the left arm toward your body and the right hand toward the audience. The cloth hangs down between them (see illustration). Lift the cloth a bit with your right hand and bring it down behind the left arm. When the right hand is hidden behind the left arm,

hook the pin into your left coat sleeve and let go. The cloth will remain hanging from your left arm and, from the front it will still look as though you are holding it up with your two hands. But actually your right hand is now completely free.

With your free right hand quickly reach inside your jacket and remove the Lotus Tree. Poke it in the dirt in the pot as you lower the cloth to hide it. PLEASE do NOT look down with your eyes even for a moment. Keep talking, looking at the audience, as though you were simply covering the pot for just a moment. This takes practice! Watch yourself in a mirror the first few times. If you look down, everyone will know you are up to something . . . don't do it. Work by feel and memory only.

As soon as the tree is in the pot return your right hand to the corner with the hook and release the pin. Twist your hands apart as you lift the cloth and show the "most beautiful flowers in the world."

Now you must be an actor. The audience laughs at your scrawny tree but you must appear to be horrified . . . remember, that is not what you claimed you would produce. The more embarrassed you appear, the more laughter you will "milk" from your audience.

Finally, sadly walk to your sign and get the final laugh by turning it around to make the GREAT MYSTO simply "mysto."

Surprisingly, later your audience will think about this trick and suddenly realize that you actually did produce a tree . . . though a scrawny one . . . in a way they do not understand. Perhaps that will puzzle them even more.

Following a comedy trick with another comedy trick is quite all right. In fact, some magicians do nothing but comedy tricks, one after another. There is the advantage that once people are in a laughing mood it is easy to keep them laughing. The next trick has been used by many magicians for many years. It is very, very funny just because the very idea of the trick is so ridiculous . . . yet it happens.

MY ASSISTANT THE CHICKEN

"I would like to conduct an EGGS-periment for you with hypnotism," declares Mysto the Magnificent as he calls his faithful assistant on stage.

"I am going to hypnotize Henry here so he will think he is a real live chicken. He will not only act like a chicken, think like a chicken, and move like a chicken, but he will be so sure that he is a real chicken that he will even lay real eggs right before your eyes!"

He brings his assistant to the center of the stage and invites him to sit in a chair. Mysto then waves his arms, speaks mysteriously, and proceeds to hypnotize Henry. Henry slouches over as though asleep, then he suddenly sits up and cocks his head. He begins to flap his arms like wings. He jumps out of the chair and begins to strut, chickenlike, around the stage. Holding his hands under his armpits he "flaps" his "elbow wings," clucks loudly, scratches the floor with his "claws," and even occasionally turns his back toward the audience and "wiggles his tailfeathers."

The audience roars with delight as Mysto chases after him trying to return him to his chair. Henry flaps and screeches as he hops away. Finally, Mysto is successful and Henry sits down in the chair again.

Standing behind his chair, Mysto orders Henry to "Lay an egg." Nothing happens.

"Perhaps he needs a little encouragement," suggests Mysto. "He probably misses his barnyard friends. Why don't you take their place?"

Mysto invites the entire audience to begin "clucking like chickens." He begins the clucking and invites everyone to join in. It's fun and the spectators soon catch the spirit and begin to cluck along.

Suddenly Henry's mouth opens slightly and the audience is amazed to see an egg inside. Mysto reaches up and removes it. He shows it and places it on a small tray on his table.

"Perhaps," he suggests, "it will work again. Let's try clucking."

The audience clucks away and another egg appears in Henry's mouth. Mysto removes it, places it on the tray and suggests the audience keep on clucking.

Time and time again an egg appears in Henry's mouth only to be removed and added to the eggs already on the tray. Finally there are eight or ten eggs on the tray. Suddenly, the assistant wakes up with a start, looks around at the audience as though he were horrified, and gets out of his chair and races offstage.

"You know," explains Mysto, "I have been meaning to take him to a doctor for some time because he is really beginning to think that he is a real chicken. I would take him, too, except for one thing. As you've probably already guessed . . . we can always use the eggs!"

The audience chuckles at this terrible joke. Mysto continues, "Perhaps you can use the eggs, too? Does anybody here need any eggs?"

The audience shouts and lets Mysto know that they do want the eggs.

"*Okay*, here," shouts Mysto as he tosses the trayful of eggs out over the audience.

"Take them home . . . and don't ever tell anyone that wasn't a good egg."

The audience screams and ducks but the eggs are all filled with confetti and break softly.

How?

You will need about 11 eggs for this trick. All but one are prepared by blowing out the insides. To do this, punch a small hole in both ends of the egg with a sharp needle. Push a piece of wire or long needle inside and wiggle it around to break the yolk; then, holding the egg over a bowl, blow hard in one end so the inside of the egg comes out the other hole. Save all the insides, because they make fine scrambled eggs! Set the blown eggs aside for a day or so until they are dry inside; then fill them with confetti or torn bits of colored paper. (Cut-up colored comic strips make good confetti.) Paste a little piece of paper over each hole to keep the confetti inside.

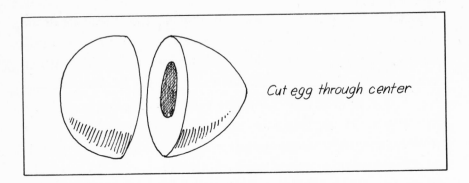

Cut egg through center

The one extra egg is prepared differently. Hard boil it (cook in boiling water for at least 20 minutes) and when it is cool, cut it right in half with a knife. Remove the inside and eat it if you like, but save the shells. One of the half shells will be most important.

Place the confetti-filled eggs in your coat pockets. Have some in the right side and some in the left side. Maybe five in each pocket, but probably fewer. Don't have your pockets obviously bulging!

Your assistant holds one of the half eggshells hidden in one of his hands. The rest is acting. The magic is easy!

Pretend to hypnotize him and have him act like a chicken. While you chase him around the stage to return him to the chair, Henry simply raises his hand to his mouth and slips the half eggshell inside. He can do this easily while he is trying to hide from you and his back is toward the audience. The shell goes in so his tongue can slip inside. In this position, it will not be difficult to keep the eggshell hidden inside his mouth and keep his face looking natural. Since he cannot say anything anymore, he should sit in the chair and appear to be hypnotized.

Invite the audience to cluck like chickens. As they do, Henry simply pokes the eggshell end out between his lips with his tongue. You are standing right behind him at this time. As the egg appears reach into your pocket and remove an egg. Your arm and pockets are completely behind Henry and the chair so nobody can possibly see you do this. Reach up quickly with this hand, keeping the hidden egg facing away from the audience and move it directly in front of your assistant's mouth. As soon as your hand is in front of his mouth he draws the eggshell back inside, and you turn your hand over to show the audience the egg. The illusion will be perfect. It will appear that you simply reached up and removed the egg that everyone saw appear a moment before in Henry's mouth.

The egg is placed on a tray and the audience is asked to continue clucking. Again, the assistant pokes out the half eggshell, and you reach into your pocket and palm a blown egg to make the switch.

You will find that, by moving your body from right to left behind the chair, you can hide either your right or left hand to "steal" an egg from either pocket.

Eight or ten eggs, done quickly, are quite enough. After that, the audience will become bored. You have convinced them that Henry can really lay eggs.

Have Henry "wake up" and run offstage as though he were embarrassed to suddenly find himself onstage.

One final thought: If you prefer to use real eggs instead of blown ones, you can. Just finish by breaking one in a glass to show it is real. The only problem, of course, is that one may break in your pocket and that can be very embarrassing for The Great Mysto!

Now Mysto is ready to finish his show. His last trick, or finale, must be one of his best. It should be a quick trick that is very surprising and showy. This will be the "dessert" . . . the last thing the audience sees. Because we often remember the last thing best, the last trick should be a knockout in a stage show. Producing a live rabbit would be a terrific finale. The audience would remember it for a long time. Mysto can do even better than that . . .

THE WISHING PAPER

Mysto picks up a sheet of newspaper from his table and opens it, showing both sides very deliberately.

"Have you ever read all the advertisements in just one page of a newspaper?" he asks. "Every time I do I call the paper my 'wishing paper' because I'm always wishin' I could have everything in it."

Mysto's assistant walks onto the stage holding a large "picture frame" of thin wood in front of him. Mysto places the sheet of newspaper over the frame and fastens it in place with thumbtacks. When this is done Mysto and his assistant hold the frame between them.

"What a lovely sheet of wishing paper," says Mysto. "Look, here's a strange ad. It says, 'free red silk handkerchief, poke here.'"

Mysto looks puzzled. "Let's try it," he suggests.

He pokes hole in the newspaper and pulls out a large red silk handkerchief.

"Look . . . here's another ad offering me a free blue one."

He pokes another hole and produces a blue silk handkerchief. The fun continues. Mysto reads ad after ad and pokes more holes. He draws out stockings, a towel, a pencil, a flashlight, a lightbulb, a necktie, a belt, a hot dog, a piece of rope, and finally, to the delight of the entire audience, he breaks through the paper and fishes around until he removes a real *live rabbit.*

Just what every magician wishes for!" announces Mysto, holding the bunny up for all to see.

"Thank you, everyone," he says as the audience applauds.

"Now that my show is over may I read you just one final wish from my wishing paper?"

He glances at the newspaper, then reads aloud:

"Remember me early or remember me late . . . but, please, never forget your friend MYSTO THE GREAT . . . and his GREAT COMPANY, TOO."

He gestures toward his assistant, who bows slightly toward the audience. As the audience applauds, and the curtains start to close slowly, Mysto and his assistant walk to the big sign that now reads:

> **mysto**
> **and**
> **company**

They pull the sign off and walk offstage, leaving a new sign that reads:

> **THE GREAT MYSTO**
> **AND**
> **THE GREAT COMPANY**

The show is finished!

How?

First, if you are worried about where you will obtain a live rabbit, don't be. You don't have to use one. In fact, you can produce any objects you wish using this same trick. The rabbit is suggested because most magicians like to know of a way to produce one.

First you must make a "picture frame." This is made from four small pieces of soft wood, like pine. Its size will depend on the size of the newspaper sheet you use. You will have to measure a sheet of your local newspaper and make the frame just big enough so the newspaper covers it completely.

To the center of the top of the frame attach a *strong* piece of dark thread. (Read further to see how long it should be.)

Roll your colored handkerchiefs into small balls and place them in small squares of newspaper. Gather the corners to make small bundles. Fasten them with a tiny piece of sticky tape. Make similar packages of the rope, belt, pencil, etc., that you choose to produce. Finally, with fine sewing thread, tie them onto the strong thread on the frame. The bundles should be attached to the string, as it hangs in the frame, from about halfway down. The small bundles are tied on so the string looks like a bunch of grapes. The illustration will make this clear.

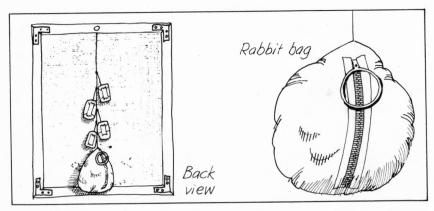

Rabbit bag

Back view

If you wish to produce a rabbit, you will require a special holder. Sew a bag of white cloth just big enough to hold the bunny. Sew a zipper in one side. Tie a big loop of string to the zipper so you can find it quickly. Later you will be able to reach through the newspaper hole and quickly unzipper the bag to draw out the rabbit.

To hide the "production items" simply have your assistant sling them over his shoulder while he holds the frame in front of him. The bundles are hidden behind his back. In this position he walks onto the stage. He must keep his back toward the back of the stage so the audience cannot see the bundles; however, he need only step a few feet onto the stage. Mysto walks over to meet him, and attaches the newspaper to the frame while the helper holds on.

Tack the paper to the frame. A hint: Have the tacks already lightly pushed into the frame so you have them when you want them. That way you won't slow the trick down by looking for the tacks.

Once the paper is in place, walk beside your assistant. Take a top corner of the frame and let him move out from behind it as he holds the opposite top corner. This allows the bundles to swing from behind his back to behind the newspaper. The frame is now held between both you and the assistant. You can walk to the front of the stage center to perform the trick.

You can look behind and see where the bundles are and then punch through the paper at the right spot to get them. It is a good idea not to have too many objects, or you may get confused.

You can punch holes in different places because the bundles are spread out along the string, and by twisting the frame a bit you can move other parts of the paper in front of the bundles. A little experimenting and practice will show you how really easy this is.

Finally, if you've decided to do it, punch a hole big enough for both hands and reach through to "unzipper" your bunny. After you draw him out, your assistant must tip the frame a bit so the bag is hidden behind the unripped part of the newspaper. Then he immediately walks offstage, drops the frame, and returns for your final "bit" with THE GREAT MYSTO sign.

As the curtains close on your stage show you also receive your graduation diploma from THE GREAT MYSTO's school of magic. You have been Mysto's "sorcerer's apprentice" through this whole book. You have learned a great deal about what a magician is and what he does. You have learned the kind of shows he can produce and the predicaments he finds himself in. You have learned to be an actor, and you now know "acting" is the magician's greatest trick. You know that magic secrets are not nearly as important as entertainment. Anyone can learn secrets, only a performer can be an entertainer.

You probably think THE GREAT MYSTO doesn't really exist. He comes closer to existing now. All you have to do is assemble your props, prepare your gimmicks, practice your effects, learn your patter, and search out places to show your stuff, and it won't be long before your friends begin to know THE GREAT MYSTO . . . and that's you!

ABOUT THE AUTHOR

Laurence B. White, Jr. is a man who is constantly bubbling over with enthusiasm, whether it be in the realm of magic or in the teaching of science. He is a popular television teacher and is a member in good standing of the S.A.M. (Society of American Magicians). Mr. White has been a performing magician since he was 13, and made all of his "spending money" in college performing magic shows for amateur nights, parties, and in the theater between shows. Assistant Director of the Needham (Massachusetts) Elementary Science Center, Larry resides in nearby Stoughton with his wife and two sons, Dave and Billy.